THROUGH THEIR SISTERS' EYES

Representations of Black Men in Some of the Early Fictions of Toni Morrison, Alice Walker, and Toni Cade Bambara

KOMLA MESSAN NUBUKPO

THROUGH THEIR SISTERS' EYES

Representations of Black Men in Some of the Early Fictions of Toni Morrison, Alice Walker, and Toni Cade Bambara

GALDA VERLAG 2018

Bibliografische Information der Deutschen Nationalbibliothek
Die Deutsche Nationalbibliothek verzeichnet diese Publikation in der Deutschen Nationalbibliografie; detaillierte bibliografische Daten sind im Internet über http://dnb.ddb.de abrufbar.

© 2018 Galda Verlag, Glienicke
Neither this book nor any part may be reproduced or transmitted in any form or by any means electronic or mechanical, including photocopying, micro-filming, and recording, or by any information storage or retrieval system, without prior permission in writing from the publisher. Direct all inquiries to Galda Verlag, Franz-Schubert-Str. 61, 16548 Glienicke, Germany

ISBN 978-3-96203-043-8 (Print)
ISBN 978-3-96203-044-5 (Ebook)

For my wife Povi, and for our children Akpe, Brice and Gila.

CONTENTS

Foreword xi
Introduction xvii

1 TONI MORRISON'S PERSPECTIVES

1.1 The Black man as a loser: *The Bluest Eye* and *Sula* 3

1.2 Choosing to Win: *Song of Solomon* 18

1.2.1 Macon Dead II, or the Pursuit of Loneliness 18

1.2.2 Milkman or the quest for self-definition 27

1.2.3 Creating a home: Guitar as a political activist 36

1.3 The divorce from the material : *Tar Baby* 42

2 ALICE WALKER'S BLACK MEN

2.1 Manhood Redefined: A Study of Alice Walker's *The Third Life of Grange Copeland* 59

2.2 The Black man in an inter-racial relationship: An approach to *Meridian* 76

2.3 Humanizing The Black Man : An Analysis of *The Color Purple* ... 90

3 BLACK MEN IN THE FICTION OF TONI CADE BAMBARA

Black Men in the Fiction of Toni Cade Bambara 109

Conclusion 125

Selected bibliography 129

FOREWORD

This book heavily depends on a number of literary and critical terms, some of which I would like to explain before I proceed. To begin with, the term "metacritical approach" in the title of this study may not seem familiar to many. Since the Enlightenment, the rise of rationality in the public sphere has remained a living reality across the world. All aspects of human life so far have been permeated by the use of reason and an art form like literature is no exception. Education consequently appears as the tool to be equipped with in order to easily access the efficient use of rationality. The critical tradition that was established long ago in the Western hemisphere keeps on getting consolidated. As far as the Black world is concerned, the empire of reason, the western style, has been gaining ground for long. The putting in place of a critical tradition has been going on in the Black world as well and every means available to them is being used by Blacks all over the world to make their own statements in a world that does not think it appropriate to value their dignity and opinions. Literature, in the context of this book, is one such means. The production of creative writings is regarded there as a way of looking back at the powerful master by the oppressed who are struggling to get across a new message. Self and the Other therefore emerge in this public sphere. The gist of this study is to critically approach an already-existing critical tradition, that is, the African American one. Metacriticism is simply the criticism of criticism. Its use in this book then implies a critical approach to how African Americans have established the values that undergird their critique of the American society that has turned out to expel them from mainstream considerations. The African American critical tradition has a strongly political facet and the metacritical approach just highlights this in this study.

By the term African American critical tradition, I mean the generally established process through which black writers and critics in the United States resist intellectually the shameful American system. This process has started out since the eighteenth century with the poems of Phillis Wheatley, a slave girl, up to date. Blacks were held slaves in the past and were not allowed to learn to read or to write. But when they got against all odds the chances to do so, they used that means to critically evaluate the hostile environment they lived in. It is crucial to note that, for African American critics, being an intellectual means devoting one's knowledge to uplifting the black race. All mischievous behaviors from the white community against Blacks have no rational grounds. It was a dominant belief among white Americans until recently that their race was superior to the black race and thus Blacks do not deserve any human treatment. This situation did not and does not match any rationality because it forces Blacks to the private sphere. It is then a must for black intellectuals to come to the public sphere to rationally criticize that and help Blacks promote new reading of their old margins. The realm of rationality which is also the realm of criticism should shed lights on all aspects of human lives, including the relationships between racial entities. The black critical tradition should then be understood as a full intellectual commitment to solving the problems of the oppressed. Through their writings, African Americans along the years have devised means and strategies to debunk all negative ideas the white-dominated society has cast on them. It is also an opportunity for African American writers to show their equal merits of acknowledgments with their white peers. As Ambroise C. Medegan notes, their primary goal is "se faire connaître en tant qu'écrivains au même titre que leurs pairs blancs et de bénéficier des gains découlant de cette reconnaissance."[1] However, the tradition is far from being a monolithic voicing of the issues opposing Blacks to Whites. Interestingly, the tradition has served to overthrow old canons that existed before. They are Caucasian canons which overlooked other realities that are different from them. However, as the African American critical tradition developed, it unconsciously incorporated some of the norms it has been combating. Before the 1960s especially, the tradition became male-dominated. Thus, writings by African American women were overlooked and dealt with less seriousness. The male writer thought he was the best person to speak for the community, only to discover that the realities of the other

---

1 Ambroise C. Medegan, "Aspects de la critique littéraire africaine américaine", in Geste et Voix, N° 6 (April, May, June 2009) p. 25

gender are actually neglected. Therefore, black females split from the group and raised specific issues by and for themselves. The tradition does not de facto constitute a destructive force against itself but has become dynamic and multi-toned. The tradition moots the specific role the African American intellectuals should play in the larger American society to uplift the black race. Critically evaluating this tradition surfaces the fact that it is difficult for Blacks in general in the United States to establish a critical tradition without having white people in their minds. Specifically, in addition, it is revealed that black women cannot establish the tradition without being conscious of (black) men. The issue of otherness has thus forcibly become central to the tradition. What then is "otherness"?

Otherness—also called alterity—is the condition of being dissimilar, strange, different, or exotic. The term is opposed to identity. Identity is a complex term, especially as we refer to the European philosophical approach to the term. Descartes and Locke are among the great thinkers who have elaborated a lot on the issue. For example, John Locke discusses identity as an invention which is rather difficult to be grabbed by human understanding. He explains this in his An Essay concerning Human Understanding II, xxvii, Of Identity and Diversity. As one can understand, we cannot talk about identity without referring to the consciousness. Consciousness of one's own being is crucial in the definition of one's identity. In the book's introduction, one can read: "La certitude de mon existence s'explicite aussitôt comme certitude de l'existence de cette « chose qui pense » que je suis."[2] By extension, a person who is conscious of his own being is also simultaneously conscious of the existence of other persons. This reality also nourishes the debate over similarity and difference. Simply put, one can feel secure with people who look or behave like oneself. Such examples can be found with people of the same age group, the same family, ethnic group, religion, sex, or race. One tends to better understand people he or she shares the same values with. The Other who simply does not belong to one's group constitutes a source of fear, a source of threat to the Self. For example, the heterogeneous largely perceive the homogeneous as different and, consequently, as a source of danger and unease. Likewise, the poor/rich, young/old, male/female contexts help highlight how one views the Other on the basis of dissemblance. The White/Black context has been largely discussed in this study. In the United States, the dominant perception within

---

2 John Locke, Identité et Différence : L'invention de la conscience (Paris : Editions du Seuil, 1998) p. 33

the white community is that Blacks are descendants from slaves and therefore are not full human beings. Black people who are victims of this shallow perception are then rejected and forced to the margins. Blacks' presence there is perceived to threaten the dominant white community. This reality casts a shock of differences wherein the Whites make norms that present Blacks as a source of potential trouble. Standards between both races are not the same and this constitutes a source of menace from one racial group to the other. More importantly, Whites believe that their whole culture is highly advanced (and aspects of it actually are) and that the cultures of people they have dominated and subjugated are to be swept aside and ignored. This issue is more highlighted by postcolonialism.

Postcolonialism is a critical theory developed by scholars that are conscious of the condition of being colonized. Weak nations have been dominated and subjugated by more powerful ones. The powerful nations trampled the rights of the dominated and imposed on them their ways of life and their languages. The colonized nations have been influenced by the discourses of their masters which they largely internalized. By extension, the idea of colonization applies to other domains in the society. The man has become the colonizer of the woman. Adults have colonized the young. The rich have subjugated the poor. The Self has stifled the Other. The postcolonial theory therefore implies the discussion about the various experiences of the colonized and their various forms of resistance to the master-colonizer. It is a process of resistance. It is a process of reconstruction too. That is, what is suppressed, looked down upon, enslaved, displaced, and differentiated has to be revisited and restored. In the African American context, this theory is a working one. It helps correct the issues of representation of black people living in the United States by their white masters. As noted by Paula M. L. Moya in her Learning from Experience, "(…) if there were no sociological distinct and identifiable groups of people such as "African Americans" who can be shown to be systematically denied access over a long period of time to economic and educational opportunities, there would be little reason to institute a government-sponsored program to redress those historical exclusions"[3]. Understandably enough, redressing the situation is very important to constructing a less biased and subjected understanding of the multicultural American community. Postcolonialism is also useful in revisiting the hidden aspects in the expression of humanity by both Blacks

---

1 Ambroise C. Medegan, "Aspects de la critique littéraire africaine américaine", in Geste et Voix, N° 6 (April, May, June 2009) p. 25

and Whites on the basis of their differences. This theory is a reformist theory which highlights the awareness rising by the colonized people and the critical strategies developed to help themselves out.

As far as the critical discourse is concerned, it can be said that the creative literature is concerned with the aesthetics—the nature of the beautiful and the judgments concerning the beauty. Creative literature prioritizes the creation of the beautiful. In this process, the world is always restructured; the art never being the textual reproduction of the world. Something is forcibly added. This is highlighted through strategies of creation of the beauty and, consciously or insidiously, one criticizes what existed before. Clearly, the newly created is a new version of the existing one. But then, what is added or removed can be perceived as a critique of what existed. The critical discourse is actually the language used for conviction purposes, the language to convey a message that convinces. When the language is ideologically marked, one can talk of discourse.

Besides, as one does a chronological reading of African American writings, some ideas and terms become recurrent. Moreover, the period of these writings covered in this book may suggest to many the idea of literary history. As a matter of fact, the literary history of this period reveals the political stance of ex-slaves who continued to fight for a true liberation of the black community, a struggle to resurrect Blacks' culture, the strategies of promoting the black race, and black women's struggle for emancipation. Issues of oppression, freedom, identity, and equality come over and over again through the fiction of African American writers and critics of the period. In addition, the study suggests also the issue of history of ideas.

History of ideas denotes the development of ideas through a given period. It is a study of how an idea or a number of ideas can be traced with the time. In the African American context, issues of otherness are central to the tradition but are not expressed in the same way. Blacks were rejected because first they were slaves. Furthermore, they were proclaimed free and could be thought of as the equals of the Whites but they were still marginalized and could not fully participate in mainstream events. Likewise, institutionalized segregation was brought to an end, which allowed Blacks to share the same facilities with the Whites but they were not given the economic means to achieve that. At a moment of their story, black women have become conscious of the fact that they have been otherized by their male counterparts. So, otherness has become a dynamic issue within the tradition.

INTRODUCTION

Although William Stanley Braithwaite's statement is evidently true that "... the Negro was *in* American literature generations before he was part of it as a creator,"[1] it fails to take note of the fact that it took the black American woman even longer than it took the black man to emerge as a creative writer. As far as fiction is concerned, by the time the first novel by a black woman was published-arguably F. E. W. Harper's *Iola Leroy* in 1892 - black male writers had already established a tradition of their own. William Wells Brown initiates black fiction, in 1853, when he publishes his first novel *Clotel or the President's Daughter*, and the foundation of the new tradition is soon consolidated by both Frank J. Webb's *Garies and their Friends* (1857), and Martin R. Delany's *Blake: or the Huts of America*, published serially from 1859 through 1861. In all three novels, black men are depicted as the victims of a socio-economic system, and black women, as their dedicated companions.

I suggest, here, that the first generation of black women novelists -- Frances E. W. Harper and Pauline E. Hopkins, to name but two -- joined this tradition without questioning the premises upon which it was founded. Black American men and women are victims of the same history; granted. And Trudier Harris is certainly right to regard that history as the major source of inspiration for Afro-American creative writers in general. In her opinion: "(t)he intensity of the historical experiences which the Black people have lived in America (...) has understandably so penetrated their literature that there are times when the two cannot be separated."[2] As a matter of fact, many black authors readily

---

[1] William Stanley Braithwaite. "The Negro in American Literature" in Addison Gayle, Jr., ed. Black Expression (New York: Weybright and Talley), 1969, p. 169.
[2] Trudier Harris. Exorcising Blackness. (Bloomington: Indiana University Press), 1984, p. ix

let find their way into the plots of their fiction, accounts of actual events. The presence, in the Afro-American text, of those –creatively speaking – unprocessed "facts" bears evidence of the American Blacks' ability to design a wide range of strategies destined to emphasize the necessity for them to humanize the hostile environment where they have been living. In the preface to Pauline E. Hopkin's *Contending Forces* (1899), the author reminds the reader that "the incidents portrayed in the early chapters of the book actually occurred. Ample proof of this may be found in archives of the courthouse at Newberne, N.C., and at the national seat of government, Washington, D. C."[3] This way of dramatizing the plight of the community gives the concept of realism a whole new meaning. By making accounts of reality part of their fictions, black writers clearly express an obsessive awareness of the condition of their people and, consequently, underline the little control blacks still have over their own lives.

To a large extent, to survive as a black person does not mean anything unless it implies surviving as a member of the black community. Ironically enough, despite the fact that the majority of black men and women in slavery were treated in the same way, the existence of conflicting functional classes among the slave population made it impossible for a unicity of perspective to prevail, among the slaves, on issues of importance to them. Among the very first African American fiction writers there existed, however, a tacit understanding of the necessity for them to harness the energies of the various interest groups in order to generate a new spirit. Little wonder that a kind of consensus can be identified in most of the first literary works produced by them. William Wells Brown's *Clotel* is not only a scathing criticism of slavery, but also an attempt to teach fellow blacks to unite as brothers and sisters. The same rhetoric of black brotherhood permeates all other novels by blacks in slavery. Even several decades after emancipation, when F. E. W. Harper wrote *Iola Leroy*, the prevailing strategy among black writers was still sustained by a philosophy of action which Houston A. Baker, Jr., in a different context, referred to as "Integrationist Poetics."[4] Black writers, both male and female, were them committed to the same goal that was the pulling together of the bits and pieces of their shattered racial dignity. To some extent, black American fiction from *Clotel* up to Pauline E. Hopkins' *Contending Forces* (1899), is

3 Pauline E. Hopkins. Contending Forces. 1899, 1900; reprinted (Miami, Fla : Mnemosyne Publishing Co ; Inc.), 1969, p. 14.
4 Houston A. Baker, Jr. "Generational Shifts and Recent Criticism in Afro-American Literature", in Black American Literature Forum. Vol. 15, Nov. 1, Spring 1981.

but a variation on the twin themes of white racism and black brotherhood. To say this is not to imply that the black community, then, never dealt with frictions within the black community. The novelists, especially the female ones, were aware of some of the internal contradictions with which the group was plagued. In that respect, F. E. W. Harper's is unquestionably a feminist perspective. She writes: "Through weary, wasting years, men have destroyed, dashed in pieces, and overthrown, but today we stand on the threshold of woman's era, and woman's work is grandly constructive"[5] Oddly enough, she dismisses sexism in the black community as a "lesser question" because, in her opinion, "being black is more precarious than being a woman."[6] This last proposition was valid then. Not anymore; that is if one looks at it in light of the creative works of Toni Morrison, Alice Walker, and Toni Cade Bambara.

Emancipation certainly met the expectations of some former slaves. However, it also generated more confusion among many black men. As a matter of fact, the objective conditions that governed the latter's lives did not change much, if at all. In addition, not many of them were psychologically prepared – or even allowed by the prevailing social and political structure – to be competitive in the context of capitalist America. Last of all, and as a result, the pattern of manhood provided by the dominant culture was almost impossible for them to follow. The full measure of the psychological trauma that these unfortunate black men went through in slavery and after, is not too hard for black women to appraise because the latter have always been around black men. One may arguably suggest that the slave system 'equipped' black women, much better than it did black men, to adjust themselves to life after emancipation. In any case, black men and black women in slavery, it seems to me, did not learn to evaluate their personal worth in the same ways. This partly accounts for the covert bipolarization that has informed the black American character since the turn of the 19th century. Black people still have the same culture but black men and black women no longer emphasize the same beliefs, opinions, concepts, values, and norms. Economics, politics, and most important, gender have become crucial factors in splitting the community into sub-groups.

---

5 F. E. W. Harper ; quoted in Hazel V. Carby, " 'On the Threshold of Woman's Era': Lynching, Empire, and Sexuality in Black Feminist Theory." Critical Inquiry, Volume 12, Number 1, Autumn 1985, p. 262.
6 F. E. W. Harper, quoted in Gloria Wade-Gayles. No Crystal Stair, (New York: the Pilgrim Press), 1984, pp. 10 - 11

In the field of creative writings, the new situation has accelerated the individualization of talent among women. By generating, in the late 1920s and early 1930s a dynamics that prepared the ground for a fairly positive reception of Afro-American fiction by American and world readers, the Harlem Renaissance overshadowed an ironical situation whereby the "successful" creative writings inspired by the black experience were produced by white authors. Harriet Beecher Stowe's *Uncle Tom's Cabin* is a case in point. Black American women eventually seized the opportunity offered by this dynamics and started overtly ignoring the black male canons. Zora Neale Hurston takes the lead by publishing, in 1937, *Their Eyes Are Watching God*. To some extent, I regard as Z. N. Hurston's spiritual daughters, the three women whose early fictions are discussed in this study.

My objective is to analyze the representations of black men in some of the early fictions of Toni Morrison, Alice Walker, and Toni Cade Barbara. More specifically, my intention in carrying out this study is to focus on the various moments when black men, turned into an object of scrutiny by these three "sisters", are "dissected" in front of the reader. To be sure, many books have so far been written-mostly by blacks - on the American black man but some of the oldest ones are either psychological analyses like W. H. Grier's and P. M. Cobbs's *Black Rage* (1968), or psycho-philosophical investigations like *The Black Self* (1974) by M. D. Wyne, K. P. White and R. H. Coop; or sociological studies like Robert Stapples's *Black Masculinity* (1984). In American critical circles there exists, however, an obvious interest in the literary images of black men. Although the dissatisfaction of black people with their images, as portrayed in most white (American) fiction, is the core theme of Sherley Ann Williams's *Give Birth to Brightness* (1972), the subject has been considered by almost every Afro-American literary critic. In a 1953 essay by Ralph Ellison called "Twentieth - Century Fiction and the Mask of Humanity,"[7] the author of *Invisible Man* has this to say about the portrait of the black man as seen through the eyes of white novelists: "Seldom is he drawn as that sensitively focused process of opposites, of good or evil, of instinct and intellect, of passion and spirituality, which great literary art has projected as the image of man."[8] Ellison's observation goes beyond a mere rejection of one-dimensional black characters and posits that only through a balanced apprehension of the black experience can novelists lend a human face to the blacks in their fiction.

---

7 In Ralph Ellison, Shadow and Act, (New York: Random House), 1964, pp. 24 - 44.
8 Ibidem, p. 26.

In James Baldwin's estimation, the fact that so many American writers fail to see this simply reflects "... with a kind of frightening accuracy the state of the mind of the country."[9] What James Baldwin calls "the mind of the country" has been redefined by Addison Gayle, Jr. as "the roots of oppression"[10] and dialectically accounts for the emergence of "the conscious black rebels"[11] that can be easily identified in most contemporary black American novelists.

Consciousness of oppression, however, does not necessarily translate into an identical set of attitudes among all black writers in America. In this respect, the following point by Seymour L. Gross is worth underlining:

> To have had it established that in literary criticism that the Negro was, in Dunbar's phrase, "more human than African," was a necessary victory, but hardly decisive insofar as literary image was concerned. In the insistence upon the Negro's similarity to all other men -which had been the rallying cry of the battlers against the literary stereotype - there lay the ironic danger of so bleaching out his personal and cultural identity that he would be stripped of his unique and tragic history, which is to say his particular humanness.[12]

The black man, just like any other human being, is the meeting point of a "general" and a "particular". If it may be relatively easy, even between people of different ideological persuasions, to agree on the "general", the "particular" for its part is much harder to define and owes a lot, for its meaning, to the goals of the defining individual. To portray the black man in fiction is, therefore, to delineate one possible form that this "particular" can take.

Toni Morrison, Alice Walker, and Toni Cade Barbara belong to the same "identifiable literary tradition"[13] which, understandably, functions as a "... matrix of literary discontinuities that partially articulate various periods of

---

9 "Notes for a Hypothetical Novel", in James Baldwin, The Price of the Ticket, (New York: Saint Martin's Marek), 1985, p. 238.
10 Addison Gayle, Jr, The Way of the New World, (Garden City: Doubleday), 1975, p. 167.
11 Ibidem, p. 167.
12 Seymour L. Gross and John Edward Hardy, eds., *Images of the Negro in American Literature*, (Chicago: The University of Chicago Press), 1966, pp. 12 - 13.
13 Barbara Smith: "Toward a Black Feminist Criticism", in Elaine Showalter, ed. The New Feminist Criticism, (New York: Pantheon), 1985, p. 170.

consciousness in the history of an African-American people."[14] This tradition owes its very existence to the determination that has consistently sustained black American women's efforts and desire to tell their own stories. As Barbara Christian puts it, "their novels are the literary counterparts of the communities' oral traditions, which in the America have become more and more the domain of women."[15] In other words, their creative writings are sustained by the same decided efforts to scrutinize the black community's past and present on the one hand, and their ability to use their insightful findings to redefine black womanhood in the American context, on the other. I suggest here that these three women's portrayals of their "brothers" represent just three slices of the Black Experience. These portrayals make more sense when considered against the background of their authors' "project" for, as Albert Hofstadter points out: "Properties by virtue of which we value objects esthetically – e.g. beauty, grace, charm, the tragic, the comic, balance, proportion, expressive symbolism, verisimilitude, propriety – always require some reference to the apprehending and valuing person …"[16] Parts of this study will, therefore, read like portrayals of black women because most of the time the (black) men Toni Morrison, Alice Walker and Toni Cade Barbara depict in their novels or short stories depend for their images on the female characters' hopes and disappointments, on their dreams and insecurities.

From F. E. W. Harper up to the three writers studied here, the black American women writers' growth has been from self-erasure to self-assertion. Since the end of the Harlem Renaissance black female writers in America have made it known that, given the perspectives on American society which they inherited from their mothers and grandmothers, they do not belong unconditionally to the side of black men or to that of white women. In other words they perceive themselves neither as BLACK women or black WOMEN but rather as BLACK WOMEN. The very name "BLACK WOMEN" – which is not to be mistaken for "Black and Women" – suggests a kind of experience that both black men and white people are far from familiar with. It stands for a perception of America that has been developed over the centuries by a specific

---

14 Hortense J. Spillers: "Cross-Currents, Discontinuities: Black Women's Fiction", in Marjorie Pryse and Hortense J. Spillers, eds., Conjuring, (Bloomington: Indiana University Press), 1985, p. 251.
15 Black Women Novelists, (Westport, Conn.: Greenwood Press, 1980, p. 239.
16 In Houston A. Baker, Jr. Blues, Ideology, and Afro-American Literature. (Chicago: The University of Chicago Press), 1984, p. 78.

group of Americans. Elizabeth V. Spelman emphasizes this specificity in the following terms:

> To say that the image of woman as frail and dependent is oppressive is certainly true. But it is oppressive to white women in the United States in quite a different way than it is oppressive to black women, for the sexism that black women experience is in the context of their experience of racism.[17]

A most important factor often evoked when black women underline the specificity of their American experience in slavery is physical rape and its psychological aftermath. As horrifying as it is, rape never prevented them from playing a crucial role in the slave community. More than anything else, what black women say they are experiencing today is emotional, psychological, as well as intellectual rape. And their "brothers" are not exonerated. Calvin Hernton calls black men's hostility towards their "sisters" a "sexual mountain." In his opinion "… black men have historically defined themselves as sole interpreters of the black experience. They have set the priorities, mapped out the strategies, and sought to enforce the rules."[18] Now, black women do realize that as a group in present day America, they have some more alternatives than their grandmothers back in slavery. On the whole they choose to fight back and consequently put up the appropriate intellectual and psychological resistance. From the early 1950s to the mid-1980, black feminism as an ideology unquestionably became the background against which black history, American politics and fiction by black American women were critically evaluated. Quite expectedly, no single theorist of black feminism over that time managed to express the full implications of their object of study. Although for the layperson women like Barbara Smith, Audrey Lorde, and bell hooks, to mention but a few, are authorities on the subject, the truth of the matter is that they even do not always seem to agree on the essential. No wonder. Ideology, as a rule, does not exist in a vacuum. The ideology of a group is more fully expressed in the daily relationships of its members with non-members.

---

17 Elizabeth V. Spelman: "Theories of Race and Gender: The Erasure of Black Women", in Quest: a Feminist Quaterly. Vol. V, n° 4 (p. 58).
18 Calvin Hernton, "The Sexual Mountain and Black Women Writers", in Black American Literary Forum. Winter 84, Vol. 18 n° 4.

This is where creative black women writers of feminist persuasion step in. By appropriating language - defined by Kimberly W. Benston as "that fundamental act of organizing the mind's encounter with an experienced world"[19] -, black feminist novelists express the necessity for them and their ability, to give a structure of their own to their chaotic existence. In the process of reclaiming their discourse simultaneously from two dominant cultures, they successfully define themselves as the cultural minority of a disinherited minority and consequently commit themselves to making their hidden history the ultimate source of the psychological strength they need if they are to grow both as individuals and as a group. Most black female writers will probably agree with Alice Walker's point that "I am preoccupied with the spiritual survival, the survival *whole* of my people. But beyond that, I am committed to exploring the oppressions, the insanities, the loyalties, and the triumphs of black women."[20] Black women novelists, therefore, are producers of a new set of values and the (black) men in their stories are just one of the many structural devices used by these authors to promote their critical awareness of who black American women actually are. James Baldwin's observation that the black American writer "is here to describe things which other people are busy to describe"[21], consequently takes a whole new meaning when applied to American black women writers. They explore the psyche of their characters in the context of their fictions. More importantly, each of the three women studied here has a story of self-creation to tell. Toni Morrison sums up the black woman's unexpected emergence in her much-quoted observation: "... she had nothing to fall back on; not maleness, not whiteness, not ladyhood, not anything. And out of the profound desolation of their reality, she may well have invented herself."[22] In the same vein, reviewing - in the preface to *The Black Woman: An Anthology* - the huge scholarship produced on the black experience by "experts" in the various domains of the sciences of man, Toni Cade Barbara dismisses most of what male psychologists, biologists, biochemists and historians have always had to say about black women. Even

---

19 Kimberly W. Benston: "I yam what I am: the topos of (un)naming in Afro-American Literature", in Henry Louis Gates, Jr., ed. *Black Literature and Literary Theory*. (New York: Methuen), 1984, p. 152.
20 In John O'Brien, ed. Interviews With Black Writers. (New York: Liveright), 1973, p. 192.
21 *The Price of the Ticket*, p. 244.
22 Toni Morrison: "What the Black Woman Thinks about Women's Lib." New York Times Magazine, 22, August 22, 1971, pp. 14-5

the available fiction fails to meet her expectations as a black woman. She says:

> I don't know that literature enlightens us too much. The "experts" are still men, Black or White. And the images of the women are still derived from their needs, their fantasies, their second-hand knowledge, their agreement with the other experts.[23]

Black women are, therefore, the sole custodians of any first-hand knowledge of their own experience. As a result, only in their own fictions can the real story of their self-creation be told. Toni Morrison also sounds positive about this when she says that "(b)lack men don't write very differently from white men."[24] About whom or what, she does not specify. At least about black women, one should guess. This opinion of hers is in perfect harmony with the implications of what Alice Walker refers to as "the ignorance of black men about black women." Elaborating on this basic idea the author of *In Search Of Our Mother's Gardens* has this to say:

> Black women are called, in the folklore that so aptly identifies one's status in society, "the mule of the world", because we have been handed the burdens that everyone else – everyone else – refused to carry. We have also been called "Matriarchs", "Superwomen", and "Mean and Evil Bitches." Not to mention "Castraters" and "Sapphire's Mama." When we pleaded for understanding, our character has been distorted; when we have asked for simple caring, we have been handed empty inspirational appellations, then stuck in the farthest corner. When we have asked for love, we have been given children. In short, even our plainer gifts, our labors of fidelity and love, have been knocked down our throats. To be an artist and a black woman, even today, lowers our status in many respects, rather than raises it: and yet, artists we will be."[25]

---

23 Toni Cade Barbara, ed. *The Black Woman: An Anthology*. (New York: New American Library), 1970, p. 9.
24 In Claudia Tate, ed. *Black Women Writers at Work*. (New York: Continuum), 1983, p.122.
25 Alice Walker. *In Search of Our Mother's Garden*. (New York: Harcourt Brace and Jovanovich), 1983, p. 237.

In assessing the plight of the black woman in America, Alice Walker understandably points an accusing finger in many directions including the black man.

Black American women write unquestionably against the background of the above mentioned set of experiences. Little wonder their representations of the black man rival and often conflict with the latter's self-portrayals. In light of the foregoing, one could infer that Paul Lawrence Dunbar's mask metaphor, often used by critics to account for white author's difficulties in getting "… an intimate knowledge of the Negro's character, mind, or tastes",[26] can apply to intra-community relationships as well and reveal a lot to black people about each other across the gender gap. On account of the historical bond of intimacy between the black man and the black woman, the latter likes to think that she knows the former much more than he is prepared to admit. How accurate her (second-hand?) image of him is depends on the perspective from which one looks. Such a question is beyond the scope of this study, but it is interesting to note that on the whole, black women writers avoid stereotyping their male Blacks.

I break Toni Morrison's male characters into three categories. *In The Bluest Eye* the author inverts the power relation that traditionally exists between husband and wife and puts Cholly Breedlove in an economic dependency the consequences of which he was not psychologically prepared to handle; by contrast, Boyboy in *Sula* seeks to strengthen his power position and - because of his wife's silence - turns into a child. I refer to both characters as "losers". In *Song Of Solomon* I see three outstanding men who were able to give shape to their own dreams despite their difficult beginnings. Although, psychologically speaking, each of them at some point of his development proves off balance in one way or another, I regard them as "winners". I see Son in the same light in *Tar Baby* where the complex relatedness of class, race, and gender is scrutinized by Toni Morrison.

Unlike Toni Morrison, Alice Walker most of the time depicts socially maladjusted black men. In *The Third Life Of Grange Copeland* the oppressive socio-economic conditions governing the lives of the Copelands eventually give way to a keen consciousness of their plight and the realization that they have more "power" than they ever give themselves credit for. Truman in

---

26 Nancy M. Tischler. *Black Masks*. (University Park: The Pennsylvania State University Press), 1969, p. 15.

Meridian goes back and forth across the psychological boundaries between his own race and that of his life in an attempt to discover where he stands. In *The Color Purple* oppression, i. e. "*the absence of choice*" as bell hooks[27] defines it, is experienced by a number of female characters as a result of men's inability to keep their domination instinct in check.

In some of Toni Cade Barbara's short stories in general and in her novel *The Salt Eaters* in particular, I see black men very much aware of the reasons why black women need to push them aside in, in order to have acknowledged black women's contribution toward the promotion of a new order within the black community.

Although I intend to focus on their images of their "brothers", I also mean to take a close look at the underlying manipulations of situations and characters each of the three authors engages in order to portray her men. There seems to exist a tacit commitment of all female characters in the three authors' works to help each other mature and as they strive to bring forth their new selves, many a time they come up against black men with broken spirits.

---

27 bell hooks. *Feminist Theory: From Margin to Center.* (Boston, Mass: South End Press), 1984, p. 5.

1

TONI MORRISON'S PERSPECTIVES

TONI MORRISON'S PERSPECTIVES

Toni Morrison, in my opinion, does not represent in her first four novels under consideration here a stereotypical image of black men. However, her major black male characters have something in common: they all are psychologically crippled. Although most of them start out purposive, the representation they usually have, at first, of their objectives in life emphasizes the negative nature of some of the forces at work around them. Now, as Monte M. Page points out: "goals function in relation to one another and in relation to subgoals as part of a hierarchically organized structure or system."[28] Toni Morrison's men are too often caught up in complex networks of goals and subgoals over which, most of the time, they do not have much control. The original hierarchy may be of their own design but, as is the case in *The Bluest Eye*, they quickly exhibit a cognitive and/or behavioral inability to mobilize the energy they need if the goals are to be reached. At times, they are made the custodians of a power they either misuse (*Sula*, and *Song Of Solomon*) or fail to use (*Tar Baby*). Whether she portrays them as losers, or as winners, or even when she disconnects them from the material, this handicap still shows in the various ways she has them handle their lives.

1.1 The Black man as a loser: *The Bluest Eye* and *Sula*

During slavery Black culture in its popular expression emphasized the slaves' material deprivation by artistically describing the hostility of the environment

---

28 In Monte M. Page, ed., *Personality : Current Theory and Research*, (Lincoln : University of Nebraska Press), 1983, p. 11

around them. It is no exaggeration, therefore, to suggest that – apart from the church – most slaves, as a result, learnt to look inside themselves or in each other's hearts for more lasting values to cherish. This humanism which Trudier Harris calls a "code of ethics" is what, "determines models for love and sacrifices that are willingly made for others."[29] Commitment to the group, either directly or indirectly, lies at the root of this set of new values. Within the black community, to fail to live up to the expectations of (a member of) the group is to devolve from Black to "nigger". The meaning of the term "nigger" depends on who uses it and when. By Afro-American standards, though, it means, most of the time, a loser. In that sense, two outstanding losers in Toni Morrison's fiction are Cholly, in *The Bluest Eye*, and Boyboy, in *Sula*.

In *The Bluest Eye*, the first conversation the author makes Claudia the young narrator recall as the story unfolds brings together her mother, Mrs McTeer, and some of the latter's women friends, and although their "dozens" focus on the facts of their everyday lives, it soon becomes apparent that the problem with which one of their "sisters" is currently plagued can be traced to a black man called Henry and whom the narrator refers to as an "old dog", i. e. "that old crazy nigger she married up with."[30] The text then moves swiftly from the particular to the more general when one woman, speaking evidently for the rest of the group, makes the point that "some men just dog." (p.15) A sense of a community of critical black women anxious to share in their individual experiences is created right away by the author, and the very fact of its existence is an indication of the women's willingness to learn to see the world through their own eyes.

The stage is set and no sooner does the "case" called Pecola appear in the picture than she provokes Mrs McTeer's anger. Although Mrs McTeer is raising two young daughters as a single parent, she has just been appointed temporary foster mother to Pecola the daughter of Pauline and Cholly Breedlove. The long lecture their mother gives Claudia and Frieda before Pecola's arrival is meant to prepare them to accept the newcomer and make her feel at home and comfortable. But Mrs McTeer intentionally tells her children much more than they need to know about Pecola's family background. Toni Morrison clearly proceeds to delineate her project: "Cholly Breedlove, then, a renting Black,

---

[29] Trudier Harris: "The Black Women Writers and Humanism"; in R. Baxter Miller; ed. *Black American Literature and Humanism*, 1981, p. 52.
[30] *The Bluest Eye*, New York: Washington Square Press, (1970), 1972, p. 15. All subsequent quotations are from the 1972 edition.

having put his family outdoors, has catapulted himself beyond the reaches of human consideration. He had joined the animals; was, indeed, an old dog, a snake, a ratty nigger." (p. 18-9).

The house is clearly presented as an index of humanity. The wealth that it synedochically stands for is the measure of that humanity. To own a house is to be able to process wealth into the power without which in Morrison's fiction black men disintegrate into nonentities. As the set of metaphors ("old dog, a snake, a ratty nigger") suggests, only losers have no home. By narrowing down the concept of "nigger" to the image she draws of Cholly, the implied author has created a new frame of reference which insists that Cholly's status as a human being depends exclusively on his performance as a provider. This is exactly one of the lessons patriarchy has been teaching us for ages. Cholly Breedlove's purchasing power does not enable him to pay for his membership of the community of humans in general and of men in particular. As a result, he is perceived by the narrator as an unintelligent person who fails, psychologically speaking, to bring the world around him under control. He is the symbol of the worst kind of failure one can experience and this symbol takes different shapes at different stages of the story. Little wonder that Pecola arrives with nothing. The fact of the matter is that she is the daughter of a "nobody" and as a result, she is perceived by Mrs McTeer as the painful presence of an unbearable absence. Pecola, consequently, has no right to drink three quarts of milk in her foster home:

> Three quarts of milk. That's what was in that ice-box yesterday. Three whole quarts. Now they ain't none. Not a drop. I don't mind folks coming in and getting what they want, but three quarts of milk! What the devil does anybody need with three quarts of milk (p. 22)

In her comment on her mother's observation, Claudia candidly notes that "the 'folks' my mother was referring to was Pecola."(p.22) The author's voice lurking behind Mrs McTeer may be indirectly talking to Pecola here but as a matter of fact, the most important implication of the message is that Claudia's mother is talking *about* Pecola's father. The end of the monologue, not surprisingly, sheds a more crucial light on Cholly:

> Folks just dump they children off on you and go on 'bout they business. Ain't nobody even peeped in here to see whether that child has a loaf of bread. Look like they would just peep in to see whether I had a loaf of bread to give her. But naw. That thought don't cross they mind. That old trifling Cholly been out of jail two whole days and ain't been here yet to see if his own child was 'live or dead. (p.23)

Although Cholly's irresponsibility is posited as a fact at the very beginning of the novel, the author keeps piling up the reasons why he should be regarded as a failure. In the foregoing quotation, the narrator allows for the implied author's project to be seen through the eyes of a woman who has to carry the burden of Cholly's mistakes. Mrs. McTeer's, however, is not just another voice telling the same story; instead, she is portrayed as the authorized voice of many black women and to her, Cholly is just a despicable absentee father. Her presence in the narrative and the discourse she subsequently generates aim to validate both the experience of the people she stands for and the language in which the latter feel more comfortable expressing that experience. Depicted in this language, Cholly stops being a vague concept and becomes a concrete living reality that Mrs. McTeer and Pauline Breedlove have to put up with.

The image we see of Cholly is mainly of a father. But he is also a husband. In either case he is bound by a contract the transgression of which once again turns him into a loser. In most novels by black male writers, the failure of black male characters to live up to their own or other people's expectations is usually depicted as the result of a concatenation of situations in which society and/or other men (both black and white) in one way or another deny them the right to succeed. Bigger Thomas in Richard Wright's *Native Son* and the invisible man in Ralph Ellison's *Invisible Man* are two cases in point. Each of them is portrayed as a product of a political and economic system or represented through the consciousness of males who are in positions of power - a power they are unwilling to lose. By contrast Toni Morrison's black men – thanks to the way their strategically conceived biographies are articulated in her works – acknowledge the existence of black women in their lives. In *The Bluest Eye* Toni Morrison allows Cholly to turn childish as a result of his manipulation by his wife. Even in *Song of Solomon* where Macon II, the tireless provider, is portrayed neither as a great husband nor as an outstanding father to his daughters, most of his life is structured around his wife. As a matter of fact, in *The Bluest Eye*, *Sula*, *Song of Solomon* and *Tar Baby* the portraits of black male characters are, not surprisingly, often painted against the background of female sensitivity. In *The Bluest Eye* and *Sula*, when black men turn out to be losers, they do so mainly as women's partners.

When Pauline and Cholly start out, they love each other. Her mental representation of Cholly prior to their marriage is informed by the dialectics of a shared love. Because he loves the woman who is in love with him, he is perceived by her to be lively, kind, funny, and straightforward. And yet, the narrator's account of those bygone days with respect to Cholly's new attitude sounds characterized by a camouflaged uncertainty. The narrator makes the point that "He seems to relish her company and even to enjoy her country ways and lack of knowledge about city things." (p. 92) If Cholly is a dedicated lover when he first meets Pauline, it is because the implied author has endowed Pauline with "qualities" that appeal to him in his future wife. The couple's marriage and their journey up to Lorain for better conditions of living constitute a key moment in the development of the character. In retrospect, Pauline cannot tell exactly "what all happened." (p.93) What happened is that the author has allowed Cholly's wife to develop a new psychological self in Lorain while Cholly remains stuck with his old rural perspectives. The one thing Pauline does know, though, is that up north black people are "no better than whites for meanness." (p. 93) The author seems to be implying many things here, one of them being that there are conditions prevailing in the South which make it "easy" for whites to be racist. When blacks are exposed to similar conditions in the North, they lose the sense of committed brotherhood they "easily" develop in the South in response to collective oppression. In Lorain, Ohio, Pauline is made to miss the brother - sisterhood feeling. Her conviction that they "make you feel like no-count" defines the social and psychological environment prevailing in the North which, at the same time, though, stands for economic and psychological freedom. The closeness of the North to "the cold but receptive Canada" emphasizes some of the contradictions that the concept of freedom implies.

In Lorain, as Pauline becomes the incarnation of both the citizen's sophisticated appearance and the individual's alienation from the community in the city, her husband struggles the best way he knows how, to keep abreast, but eventually disintegrates into a failure. Important as it is, Pauline's self-fulfillment in Lorain is a "subgoal" in relation to the happiness of the couple, which was the original goal they came up north to achieve. By letting the woman's subgoal outgrow the couple's goal, the author has created in Cholly a psychological imbalance. Watching Pauline grow from an innocent country girl into a sophisticated city woman, one understands the opinion that in *The Bluest Eye* Toni Morrison "dramatizes the destructive power implicit in the control of various symbolic systems."[31]

At the very beginning, money is depicted by the author as a major concern. Cholly's attitude toward Pauline's pursuit of city happiness is sustained by the fact that she is an individual capable of reaction to society's pressure in her own way. To stick to the old way is to refrain from disrupting the order that serves Cholly's purpose. Confronted by sex and gender as sophisticated city people experience them, he displays his ignorance about both. The author makes him perceive the culture drilled into women by society and tradition as the "normal" order of things. This is why he reacts to the change in his wife at first as a confused man losing ground. No wonder. In the process of learning to become a city lady, Pauline proves to be a burden to Cholly who finds her new ways rather expensive. Her preoccupation with her external looks contrasts with the moral decay she allows to take place inside her. Her new self is a cynical combination of a desire to attract black women's attention in Lorain and the willingness to use manipulation to achieve this goal. Cholly Breedlove is the first victim of this strategy. The only resistance he can put up at first in order to slow down Pauline's rapid transformation originates from his position as the only wage-earner of the couple. In that respect, by seeking and finding employment Pauline has attained the same power as her husband. Once again, the author gives Pauline both the chance and the means to achieve more visibility while the old symbols from which Cholly used to derive his power and authority command less and less respect. When he was the only wage-earner in the home, he could afford to be the head of the family and dictate to his wife. Viewed from this angle, their journey up north-almost against her will - is a kind of psychological rape that Pauline was put through. As a wage-earner, Cholly's wife has engaged in reversing what Madonne Miner calls "...the powerful dynamics behind (the) allotment of presence/absence, language/silence, reason/madness along sexual lines".[32]

In the narrator's presentation it is mentioned that "Money became the focus of their discussions, hers for clothes, his for drink."(p. 94) The character

---

31 Keith Bayerman. *Fingering the Jagged Grain*. (Athens: University of Georgia Press), 1985, p. 185.

32 Madonne Miner: " Lady No Longer Sings the Blues : Rape, Madness, and Silence in *The Bluest Eye*." In Marjorie Pryse and Hortense J. Spiller, eds. *Conjuring: Black Women, Fiction, and Literary Tradition*, Bloomington, University of Indiana Press, 1985, p. 181.

Cholly as the author now sees him is under stress. That he opts for alcohol as a "cure" for it is indicative of a deficiency in his behavioral and cognitive coping system. As his will to keep his life under control dwindles, his portrait as seen by Pauline reads progressively like the story of her own insecurities. "Cholly," she claims, "commenced to getting meaner and meaner and wanted to fight me all the time." By processing Cholly's stress into anger, the author indicates that the character feels treated unfairly by his wife. This realization, however, does not lead him to take any positive action likely to help him to recover his human dignity. While her helplessness is presented as both the cause and the result of his newly developed drinking problem, his meanness is quickly confirmed by his attempts to depend financially on his working wife.

In contriving the plot the way she does, Toni Morrison prepares the ground for a further disintegration of Cholly as Pauline's husband. Her white mistress's advice to Pauline that it is her "husband's duty to pay the bills …" constitutes an important shift in the point of view. The issue under discussion is considered from the perspective of a representative of the dominant culture. The author suggests an alternative Pauline is not prepared to opt for because it does not serve the purpose of the author's project. Not only is Pauline unable to see any similarity between her own addiction to clothes and her husband's addiction to alcohol but the fact that she is now being advised by a white woman not to let her husband depend on her financially leads one to believe that both women, to a certain degree, have the same idea what a husband must be like. The white woman's alternative solution to the situation is divorce whereas Pauline prefers to stay on with Cholly.

From the choices Morrison imposes on the two women, one can easily infer that she intends to carry her project one step further: Pauline stays married to Cholly in order for the author to finish off establishing that he is a loser. In either case Cholly is perceived as a deviant husband. Oddly enough, when she tells him about her pregnancy, he surprises her "by being pleased." One may wonder why Cholly the alcoholic and the woman beater is, all of a sudden, happy to have a child. This surprising attitude which, at first, contrasts sharply with all that has been said so far about Cholly has a temporarily positive effect on the couple's married life in the sense that it brings both husband and wife together by sustaining the sudden hope for a better common future. Needless to wonder, though, why the author destines this couple to have children while there is every indication already that the would-be father is a psychologically crippled man who cannot even handle life with his wife. It becomes clearer that the author means to have Cholly reach the bottom of the ditch. Viewed from that perspective, Cholly's happiness at the "good" news fully makes sense. The narrator insists that "the aspect of married life that dumbfounded him and rendered him totally dysfunctional was the appearance of children." (p. 126) The scientific language used here situates Cholly, once again, below the norm. Fatherhood is, therefore, meant to bring his psychological confusion to the fullest. The same psychological confusion is expressed through indifference towards his own son by Louis – another black man – during his very brief appearance in the novel. (p. 72) The children, Sammy and Pecola Breedlove, are later on used by their mother to put their father further down. Her callous decision to "avenge herself on Cholly by forcing him to indulge in the weaknesses she despises" testifies to her preoccupation with projecting her fears into a despicable "other" on whom she can blame most of her own shortcomings. She actively participates in his disintegration by carefully monitoring her own social activities. As a result of her determination, Cholly becomes the ultimate "model of sin and failure." (p. 104) In fact, Cholly is dragged into a personality conflict by his wife who progressively manages to reduce him to a nonentity. He is the "case" married to a woman with a strategy which consists in using every asset at her disposal to show the whole world how sharp the contrast is between them:

> All the meaningfulness of the life was in her work. For her virtues were intact. She was an active church woman, did not drink, or smoke, or carouse, defended herself mightily against Cholly, rose above him in every way, and felt she was fulfilling a mother's role conscientiously when she pointed out their father's faults to keep them from having them, or punished them when they showed any slovenliness, no matter how slight, when she worked twelve to sixteen hours a day to support them. (p. 102)

Pauline's shallow preoccupation with appearance now goes beyond her original taste for nice clothes. Just as she shows off her new dresses, so has she to exhibit moral and social values that make her an attractive woman – only on the outside. Her ultimate goal being to dwarf her husband while seducing the world around them, she makes endurance a price she is fully prepared to pay. Motherhood has given her a unique chance to articulate in a whole range of ways her hatred for herself and for Cholly. Pauline's active contribution to the disappointing image of Cholly is so emphasized we eventually see him as the reflection of her negative thoughts. Considering that Cholly himself was once a victim of child abuse, the irony here is that his wife has been making every effort to reproduce the cycle of paternal irresponsibility. While Sammy and Pecola are growing up, Pauline makes sure they see their father as the living example of what they must not become. Cholly is portrayed in terms of his shortcomings. As an outcast in his own home, there is no way he can connect and communicate with his own children. Despite his wife's strategy to isolate him, however, their children in general and Pecola in particular love him. But Cholly is not even equipped – either emotionally or morally – to respond to his daughter's love. When the narrator probes into his mind one day right before he sexually abuses her, Cholly is confronted with his own uncertainties: "What could his heavy arms and befuddled brain accomplish that would earn him his own respect, that would in turn allow him to accept her love?" (p. 127) The irony of the whole story takes up a most shocking form here. Cholly has turned into a monster and his transformation has been monitored exclusively by his wife whose commitment to the pursuit of the values of the dominant culture has prevented her from fully grasping the consequences of her endeavors. She runs away from her old self for the same reason Pecola wishes she had blue eyes.

Lagging far behind his wife's new self, Cholly continues groping for the woman he used to be in love with. For a few moments, the author makes him find her in his daughter. To claim, as one critic does, that Pecola's "... father's life is a study in rejection and limitation caused and intensified by poverty and blackness,"[33] is to overlook the very active role played by Pecola's mother in the disintegration of Cholly's character. Despite the moral transgression he is guilty of, his image as a villain is simply the appearance behind the reality of Pauline's misuse of power and authority. Whatever the perspective from which one looks at the character Cholly in *The Bluest Eye*, he is portrayed as a psychologically handicapped man. To call him a loser who has no control whatsoever over his own life is to look at him from Pauline's perspective. Cholly's limitations are depicted in the context of female manipulation, which is what distinguishes *The Bluest Eye* from novels like Richard Wright's *Native Son* and Ralph Ellison's *Invisible Man*.

Cholly's life in Lorain, Ohio, is a metaphor for the community's inability to sense the full implication, for its survival, of the personal tragedies involved in

---

33 Dorothy H. Lee, "The Quest for Self : Triumph and Failure in the Works of Toni Morrison" in Mari Evans, ed., *Black Women Writers* (1950 - 1980), Garden City, N. Y., Anchor Press/ Doubleday, 1984, p. 347.

too quick an identification with the dominant culture. In Sula, Toni Morrison carries the analysis one step further by giving her black male characters the chance to experiment their own ideas. This experimentation, however, takes place in an environment polluted by racism and prejudice, which places serious limitations on the characters' performance as individuals.

The opening chapter of Sula is a romanticized description of the Bottom prior to its destruction in order "to make room for the Medallion City Golf Course." (p. 3) This is not to suggest that the Bottom used to be a sorrow - free neighborhood. The black people living up there simply managed to turn it into a celebrated place where the sense of stability that they derive from the long history of their survival justifies their attachment to it.

On the whole, the lives of the black men in *Sula* are designed by the author in the image of the township. Each of them is not satisfied with the stability that characterizes their beginnings. As a result, change has to take place. Like the road and the golf court which testify to man's willingness to achieve something concrete and lasting by taming the forces of nature, Morrison's black men, here, long to depart from their old selves in an attempt to get rid of the sense of worthlessness that the environment drills into them. Jude's personal odyssey is just an illustration of one aspect of the psychological imbalance from which they suffer as a result of the frustration they experience on different planes. When he was twenty, Jude "wasn't really aiming to get married" and the reason as articulated by the narrator is that "... although his job as a waiter at the Hotel Medallion was a blessing to his parents and their seven other children, it wasn't enough to support a wife." (pp. 80 - 81) In view of the context of Jude's life, the author's masculinist idea that a wife needs to be "supported" by her husband can be traced only to the influence of the dominant culture that Morrison partly depicts in her fiction. The narrator, therefore, conveys the sense that there is a side to Jude that is committed to the "old" value. To this arguably caring, "old" Jude who has been working so far to other people's satisfaction, Morrison opposes a "new" Jude who wants to achieve some kind of lasting recognition by attaching his name to the new road under construction:

> Along with a few other young black men, Jude had gone down to the shack where they were hiring. Three old colored men had already been hired, but not for the road work, just to do the picking up, food bringing and other small errands. These old men were

close to feeble, not good for much else, and everybody was pleased they were taken on; still it was a shame to see those white men laughing with the grandfathers and shying away from the young black men who could tear that road up. The men like Jude who could do the real work. Jude himself longed more than anyone else to be taken. Not just for the good money, more for the work itself. He wanted to swing the pick or kneel down with string or shovel the gravel. His arms ached for something heavier than trays, for something dirtier than peelings; his feet wanted the heavy work shoes, not the thin-soled black shoes that the hotel required. More than anything he wanted the camaraderie of the road men: the lunch buckets, the hollering, the body movement that in the end produced something real, something he could point to. "I built this road," he could say. (pp. 81 - 82)

Through the use of allegory, Morrison establishes that the hiring white men feel threatened by black men like Jude, which is why they prefer the old, feeble "grandfathers" over the "young black men who could tear that road up." The job satisfaction that Jude could have derived from the position he is denied is crucial to his self-fulfillment as an individual. In other words, not only does the prevailing social and economic system aim to confine blacks to the menial jobs, but in the process, young black men like Jude are stripped of their manhood. Building the new road is the ultimate affirmation of manhood as Jude sees it. To be excluded from this manly adventure is to be reduced to the status of "a waiter hanging around a kitchen like a woman." (p. 83) By suggesting this kind of comparison, the author seems to insinuate that Jude regards women as the worthless other.

Paradoxically enough, Jude survives his rejection as a psychologically diminished person fully aware that he must compensate for his low self - esteem - only by turning to a woman. Women mean a lot more to him than he is aware of. Morrison portrays him as a wounded self who, more than anything else "wanted someone to care about his hurt." (p. 8) By creating a discrepancy between the young man's real intention in marrying Nel and the latter's genuine desire "to help" and "to soothe,'" (p. 83) Toni Morrison not only makes Jude the right partner for her but, at the same time, she allows for Nel to be violated by a callous Jude Green who, as his name seems to indicate, has some more growing to do if he is to understand the true meaning of Nel's commitment to him. Jude's ultimate goal is to be a man among fellow men no matter the conditions imposed on him by white-controlled society. As a result of the author's manipulation of the context, his "frustrations become self-pity which Nel is expected to nurse, in both senses of healing and feeding."[34] To put it more bluntly: "he wants Nel to enlarge his life, even if it means diminishing her own."[35] In this respect, both Jude's affair with Sula, years later and his resulting departure from Medallion make him a failure, although of a different type than Boyboy.

Boyboy, Eva's husband and the father of her three children, has been known to be a hard working father and husband until he decides unexpectedly one day to get away from it all. During the five years of what the narrator calls a "sad and disgruntled marriage," (p.32) the character Boyboy as the author sees him is but a patchwork of negative behavior patterns. Just like Nel's husband, Eva's spouse is portrayed in terms of his limitations.

> During the time they were together he was very much preoccupied with other women and not home much. He did whatever he could that he liked, and he liked womanizing best, drinking second, and abusing Eva third. (p. 32)

As in *The Bluest Eye* where, soon after the beginning of the story, the reader is told what (s)he should perceive Cholly as, so is Boyboy's psychological and social image in Sula clearly defined and communicated by the author even before he appears on the scene. The narrator's conviction that Boyboy does whatever he likes identifies immediately the character as an unusual person in the sense that his behavior conflicts with his wife's expectations in terms of the rules and social conventions married people are supposed to live by. To go around trying to have one's way is, sometimes, to ignore not only that one is a member of a given society but also that one interacts with other people on a daily basis. The narrator's emphasis on the bad things Boyboy does and her silence about whatever good things he might do, at least once in a while, convey the author's intention to represent Boyboy as a loser. At some point, his status as a loser is even quantified when the narrator uses the language of mathematics to describe it: "When he left in November, Eva had $1.65, five eggs, three beets and no idea of what or how to feel." (p.32) Boyboy's refusal

---

34 Keith Bayerman *Fingering the Jagged Grain*, Athens, University of Georgia Press, 1985, p. 197.
35 Gloria Wade-Gayles *No Crystal Stair*, New York, The Pilgrim Press, 1984, p. 191

either engage in opportunism of outsmart everyone else. Macon Dead stands for a shrewd combination of both alternatives. Not only does Macon II have a very clear idea what he wants but in addition he is characterized throughout the novel as both a fast learner and a determined man who intends to stay in business. Quite expectedly, the author confronts him with the fact that struggling to stay in business at whatever cost has some disadvantages to it, especially if one is a black landlord with black tenants.

By moving the setting from the rural South to the urbanized North, the author anticipates new problems her black community must now prepare to face. The town is seen as a place where physical nearness in most cases comes inevitably with social distance. Macon soon develops a reputation as a callous landlord with no sympathy at all for his destitute clients. "A nigger in business is a terrible thing to see," (p. 22) says Mrs Bains a black woman tenant of his. Once again, the semantic field covered here by the term "nigger" clearly goes beyond the derogatory connotation that it has when used by white people. Its usage here relates Mrs Bains to the black oral tradition and illustrates what Henry Louis Gates, Jr. terms "(t)he ironic reversal of a received racist image of the black as simianlike, the Signifying Monkey – he who dwells at the margins of discourse ..."[36] Mrs Bains is the voice of the destitute blacks suffering from an unforgivable ruthlessness that qualifies Macon II for dismissal from the poor section of the black community – in Mrs Bains' opinion, that is. In Toni Morrison's presentation, the poor blacks' perception of the successful businessman places Macon Dead II one step closer to a white world he is more than glad to identify with, if only because it compensates for his erasure elsewhere. The story about his office substantiates his invisibility. Is this space actually his? Originally he thought it was:

> But the plate-glass window contradicted him. In peeling gold letters arranged in semicircle, the business establishment was declared to be Sonny's Shop. Scraping the previous owner's name off was hardly worth the trouble since he couldn't scrape it from anybody's mind. His store - front office was never called anything but Sonny's Shop, although nobody now could remember thirty years back, when, presumably, Sonny did something or other there (p. 17).

---

[36] "The blackness of blackness : a critique of the sign and the Signifying Monkey" in Henri Louis Gates, Jr. ed. *Black Literature and Literary Theory*, New York, Methuen, 1984, p. 286.

In fact, Macon II as the author conceives him is strong enough to ignore whatever people think about him. More exactly, he is strong enough to pretend that he does not care what people in general and fellow blacks in particular think about him. The truth of the matter is that, throughout the narrative, he is portrayed as someone who needs attention. Viewed from that perspective, his inability to have his name associated with his office in people's minds causes him psychological dissatisfaction more than anything else. The fact that "he defines himself and others by accumulation of alienated property"[37] accounts for his preparedness to endure whatever it takes to get his message across. As long as his business is thriving, his preoccupation is with strengthening his position, enjoying the fruit of his "labor", and internalizing middle-class social values. Once, he even did all three at the same time by marrying Ruth Foster. Macon seduced "the most important Negro in the city" (p. 22) into marrying off his daughter to him because at "twenty-five, he was already a colored man of property." (p. 23) Structurally speaking, the author uses this marriage as a device to boost Macon's ego by winning him some attention.

The background of the doctor whose daughter is at stake is partly painted as the victory of ethnic determination over national politics. Throughout the novel, the author emphasizes the role of money in boosting black ego. The black community in town name a street for Dr. Foster: they call it Doctor Street and later on rename it Not Doctor Street when the city administrative authorities issue a warning that the street Dr. Foster works on is not to be called Doctor Street. This determination in the black community to celebrate at all cost a successful member of the group has turned Dr. Foster into a myth. For Macon, he is a lion. And he knows that he can tame this lion by means of material wealth. The lion metaphor swiftly turns Macon who tames the "animal" into a folk hero in the narrator's words: "to lift the lion's paw knocker; to entertain thoughts of marrying the doctor's daughter was possible because each key represented a house which he owned at the time." (p. 22) Macon's property provided him with the psychological courage he needed the day he approached Dr. Foster for permission to date Ruth. The lion's response – "I don't know anything about you other than your name, which I don't like, but I will abide by my daughter's preference…." (p. 23) – at first sounds contemptuous although not discouraging. But when one scrutinizes it against the background of the narrator's observation that "In fact the doctor knew a

---

37 Keith Bayerman, *Fingering the Jagged Grain*, Athens, the University of Georgia Press, 1984, p. 201.

good deal about him and was more grateful to this tall young man than he ever allowed himself to show, " (p. 22) it becomes clear that material success means the same thing to Macon Dead and Dr. Foster. That the author makes the young man "tall" is, maybe, not a coincidence.

Both men seem happy about this marriage but obviously for different reasons: not only is Dr Foster very pleased by the fact that he is not giving his daughter to a failure – which spares him a lot of embarrassment – but in addition, he does not have to find out about the nature of a confusing attraction to his own daughter. As for the self-taught Macon II who can use, in a most creative way, the language of acquisition that nobody ever had to formally teach him, he did not marry up for the sole sake of climbing into a social class he was not born into. He married Dr Foster's daughter because, more than anything else, he wanted a Dr Foster among his business relations. Ruth's marriage is presented as a transaction between two men, i.e. a deal she is no party to. The issue of women's invisibility – a recurrent motif in Morrison's works – is raised again. The fate of the commodified Ruth is shown to be at the mercy of two men. In the Erie Lackawana episode (p. 72) it appears quite clearly that Macon II's hatred for his wife can be traced to Ruth's refusal to influence her father into lending her husband the money the latter needed then for the transaction.

So far, Macon II has been characterized by the author as a callous, selfish man who loves to cause things to happen. He symbolizes the inventiveness of the needy on their way from the periphery to the core of mainstream American society. The character's psychology unfolds along the hazy dividing line between the black community as a cultural entity and the rest of American society. Macon engages in an irreversible pursuit of loneliness and he feels comfortable using everybody as a means to his selfish end. Almost every aspect of his lifestyle testifies to his alienation from the black community. His public life is like a show-room. A show-room with a backyard to it. The strange thing about Macon II is that even in the privacy of his married life, he tends to live up to his public standards. He dutifully hides his true self from his family by developing a cold and distant attitude everybody is supposed to put up with. Although his wife is the major focus of his disdain, his children, time and time again, are also characterized as mere instruments in his tool box. The weekly rides in his Packard gives him the opportunity to exhibit his unchallenged success:

> These rides that the family took on Sunday afternoons had become rituals much too important for Macon to enjoy. For him, it was a way to satisfy himself that he was indeed a successful man." (p. 310)

Both the car and the rides evidently read like old symbols progressively acquiring new meanings and values. Macon's commitment to creating and promoting these new values overlooks the fact that for the latter to materialize, the price to be paid is a further disintegration of the black community. Ironically enough, as a nouveau riche, Macon is not rejected by the entire black community. Instead, some of them are impressed with him because his very existence emphasizes the fact that blacks also can "make it" in America. They evidently claim him as one of them and readily turn a blind eye to the clever way in which he manipulates the symbols of his success in view of conveying a sense of his newly established difference.

> Some of the black people who saw the car passing by sighed with good-humored envy at the classiness, the dignity of it. In 1936 there were very few who lived as well as Macon Dead did. Others watched the family gliding by with a tiny bit of jealousy and whole lot of amusement, for Macon's green wide Packard belied what they thought a car was for. He never went over twenty miles an hour, never gunned his engine, never stayed in first gear for a block or two to give pedestrians a thrill. He never had a blown tire, never ran out of gas and needed twelve grinning ragged-tailed boys to help him push it up hill or over to a curb. No rope leaped on his running board for a lift down the street. He hailed no one and no one hailed him. There was never a sudden braking and backing up to shout or laugh with a friend. No beer bottles or ice cream cones poked from the open windows. Nor did a baby boy stand up to pee out of them. He never let rain fall on it if he could help it and he walked to Sonny's Shop-taking the car out only on these occasions. (p. 32)

In the above passage, the semiotically coded socio-economic status of the blacks and the resulting practice they engage in is used by the narrator as the chaotic background against which Macon is writing his success story. From the confrontation between the individual and the group emerges the certainty that only the community stands for life. The background is all the noisier and livelier as the successful Macon wants to detach himself from it. By stepping back from the black community, he creates a space where he can write only the story of his cultural disconnection.

Part of the picture has something lifeless to it that close scrutiny reveals. Even the motion of the car is but faked life. Earlier on, in Macon's married life, Lena and First Corinthians – more precisely "their roving eyes" (p. 32) as the narrator suggests – were the only source of life in the whole picture. Both daughters are also regarded as non-entities. The fact of the matter is that he wishes to have, instead, a son that he can shape into his alter ego. It took him fifteen years to see this dream come true and the mistery around Milkman's conception as well as his nickname, spoils the father's joy. By refusing to let Macon know why his son is called "Milkman" by everyone, the author once again creates a psychological imbalance in the character Macon, Jr.. To give names is to give structure to what otherwise would be chaotic existence. It is to construct and reinforce a reality by designing an order and designating in specific terms the people as well as the things who go where and when within that order. In summary, through her action which leads to the coining of the name "Milkman" Ruth defies not only Macon II's history but also the very language by which he keeps his world in order. The difficult father-son relationships that the narrator dwells on eventually lead to an important turning point in the novel when Milkman hits his father for physically abusing his mother. "Macon was so shocked at being assaulted he could not speak. He had come to believe, after years of being the tallest man in every gathering, that he was impregnable." (p. 67) Just like in Sula where Toni Morrison calls Jude a "woman" because he cannot afford to exhibit "manhood" as she understands it, the "new" Macon is "reduced" to an "impregnable" person. The depiction of human frailty and the energy humans in general and men in particular devote to hiding it are signs of Milkman's future rise and fall.

Prior to this major event, the character Macon is depicted as a man of action, full of life and energy. He was constantly in control and his people, back then, used to crawl and tremble before him. Things have just changed. "Now he (creeps) along the wall looking at a man who is as tall as he (is) – and forty years younger." (p. 67) Despite the narrator's emphasis on the age difference, there is every indication that Macon could have hit his son back – on the spot that is. But he knows better. Despite all the influence he had on Milkman, Macon used to feel that his wife robbed him of his son. And unexpectedly, the latter has just taken a stand as a mature man. Through that act, "his only one" (p. 120), Milkman reminds Macon that his son is not a total failure. As a father, Macon cannot help appreciating his son's statement although he knew for sure that Milkman operated the way he did through mere lack of knowledge.

> Just as the father brimmed with contradictory feelings as he crept along the wall – humiliation, anger, and the grudging feeling of pride in his son – so the son felt his own contradictions. There was the pain and shame of seeing his father crumple before any man – even himself. Sorrow in discovering that the pyramid was not the five - thousand - year old of the civilized world, mysteriously and permanently constructed by generation after generation of hardy men who died in order to perfect it, but that it had been made in the backroom at Sears, by a clever window dresser, of papier-mache, guaranteed to last for a mere lifetime. (p. 68)

By creating the confrontation between father and son, the author has set the stage for a silent dialogue between the two characters. "Listening" to the dialogue, the reader has an idea what kind of psychological trauma both sides are going through. Milkman wishes he had not lived to see the day everything his father ever stood for must collapse. But contrary to what the son was anticipating, the father transforms in a most creative way the difficult situation facing him into an opportunity to win his son back. Instead of responding physically to Milkman's aggression, he hits his son back with his (Macon's) truth. The lecture he gives Milkman is concisely summed up in the opening statement: "You a big man now, but big ain't nearly enough. You have to be a whole man. And if you want to be a whole man, you have to deal with the whole truth." (p. 70) The language of straightforward communication is used here to convey the message that when human action is sustained by a conscious recognition of "the whole truth" it produces more lasting fruit than when it is impulsively carried out on the spur of situations. Milkman's audacity, however, helps his father open up. Throughout the novel he is portrayed as a lonely man. He has neither friends nor social life. His family life is all the less exciting as it is a boring repetition of rituals that do not mean much to the rest of the family. With this incident, things have suddenly changed. He has now in his house somebody worth talking to and he intends to seize the opportunity. Macon Dead II then continues to release onto Macon Dead III's young shoulders the burden of his long-kept secret. In so doing, he imposes on Milkman the role of a truth-carrier. In other words, Milkman becomes the meeting point of the past and the future. His father has just informed him so he can, later on, inform another generation of people.

It is important to note that this event marks the beginning of a new era in the lives of all people concerned. Macon II understandably opens the avenues of communication between himself and his son. Oddly enough, the crucial conversation between the men also marks the beginning of the erasure of Macon II from the novel. No wonder. As a rule, Toni Morrison's male characters in the novels discussed here are psychologically maladjusted and Macon is no exception. His confrontations with his son has made him gain back his balance. The nickname "Milkman" pushes aside the young man's real name "Macon." Consequently, it also dismisses as unworthy of attention the father who wanted his own dreams for the future reflected in his son. In brief, by winning back his son, the father has brought forth Macon Dead III.

In many respects, *Song of Solomon* is about people caring about themselves as much as it is about people caring about (their) people. The novel seeks to strike a balance between both poles of attraction, namely loving oneself and loving one's people, and despite their radically different perspectives on how to go about loving one's people, Milkman and Guitar, among others, are also committed to that same ideal.

1.2.2 Milkman or the quest for self-definition

In many situations, Toni Morrison has suggested in her novels that the lack of (good?) role models in their homes during their younger years partly accounts for the deficiency of the coping mechanisms of many of her black male characters. To a large extent, *Song of Solomon* is dedicated to all fathers. The opening statement: "The fathers may soar/ and children may know their names" seems to convey the urgency of the duty of black men in America with respect to the up-bringing of their children in general and of their sons in particular. In Toni Morrison's novels over the time period considered here, most black sons have been deprived of the crucial support system a father is traditionally supposed to provide. They grow up in a society –American society as a whole – which tacitly expects them to do a great job of raising themselves. The self-made individual commands a lot of respect in almost all traditions the world over ; but a person who "makes it" from scratch is not necessarily more of a hero than someone who manages to move out of an imposed frame of action in order to develop a self of his/her own choosing. Milkman has tried to do just that. Unfortunately, when he eventually decides to free himself from his almighty father in order to stand on his own feet – psychologically speaking – he gets caught between two warring factions with each side seeking to impose a type of truth on him. To make the point that Macon finally finds in Milkman someone worth talking to as I did earlier on is not to suggest that Milkman is prepared to give the answer his father anticipated.

Milkman emerges in his father's life almost as an unwanted child planned for solely by both Milkman's mother and aunt. And while Ruth Foster regards her only son as "the one aggressive act brought to royal completion" (SOS p. 133) by her, there is every indication in the father's behavior toward him that by accepting him, Macon simply wants to make the best out of a bad situation. From Macon's perspective, Milkman is a problem to which he (Macon) is the solution. The passing of values from father to son requires a scrupulous selection which, in the case of the Deads, conflicts later on with the young man's independence of spirit. Macon does not value extended family ties; nor does he believe in college education for boys.

There was a time when education used to be viewed within the black community as one of the very few ways out of poverty and into mainstream American society. This trend seems to have changed over the generations. Harold Cruise in his *The Crisis of the Negro Intellectual* traces one of the major reasons for the black people's loss of interest in education to the fact that college education only alienates black men from the black community without necessarily giving them access to white society. Educated black men only become members of a community of scholars – black and white – whereas educated whites can afford to belong to both the academic community and the white community. This is not, however, the dilemma the author thinks Macon has to solve on behalf of his son. He does see concretely what Milkman can gain by joining him in his business whereas whatever he can get going to college is too abstract and vague. No wonder he prefers to take care of his daughters' formal education by sending them to college. When it comes to his son, Macon is unequivocally for owning things.

As a young teen-ager, Milkman knows from some of his peers' perception of him that something is wrong with his father's philosophy of life. Macon's actions put Milkman in a most uncomfortable position as far as the young boy's insertion into the black community is concerned. The feeling of frustration that Milkman experiences deep down in his heart is slightly alleviated by Guitar's point that "he (Milkman) can't help who his father is." Milkman himself is brought progressively by the author to understand that he can, instead, help himself. Nevertheless, this realization fails to equip the young adult with the appropriate psychological courage he needs if he is to stop being his father's shadow. The fact of the matter is that, despite all his wishes, Milkman more than loves his father. He "... feared his father, respected him, but knew (...) that he could never emulate him." (p. 62) Because Macon is a "perfect" father, he is put too high by the author for a son like Milkman to pull down. As the saying goes, 'if you cannot beat them, join them.' After joining his father's business, he eventually devises a strategy which ironically consists in his differing from Macon only on issues of minor importance. The result is a pitiful celebration by Milkman of his own helplessness:

> Macon was clean-shaven; Milkman was desperate for a moustache. Macon wore bow ties; Milkman wore four-in-hands. Macon didn't part his hair; Milkman had a part shaved into his. Macon hated tobacco; Milkman tried to put a cigarette in his mouth every fifteen minutes. Macon hoarded his money; Milkman gave his away. But he couldn't help sharing with Macon his love of good shoes and fine tin socks. And he did try as his father's employee, to do the work the way Macon wanted it done. (SOS pp. 62 - 63)

The stubborn and conscious effort on the part of Milkman to look different from his father shows how vain the attempt is. As a matter of fact, he agrees with his father on the essential; in that he submits himself to his father's will as far as his job goes. The juxtaposition of the oppositions recorded by the language of the narrator leads to the realization that despite all his apparent efforts to be his own person, the young man likes walking in his father's shoes. And yet, as the crises add up in Milkman's life, the character is seen reaching out for help. By acknowledging his own limitations in a more responsible way, he allows room for in-depth improvement in his life as well as in that of his people. The first major crisis – his hitting his father – sets in motion a chain reaction. Milkman, right away, discovers that even if he is not, physically speaking, a changed person, deep down in his soul something very important has just happened. He ...

> ...stood before his mirror and glanced, in the low light of the wall lamp, at his reflection. He was, as usual, unimpressed with what he saw. He had a fine enough face. Eyes women complimented him on, a firm jaw line, splendid teeth. Taken apart, it looked all

> right. Even better than all right. But it lacked coherence, a coming together of the features into a total self. It was all very tentative, the way he looked, like a man peeping around a corner or some place he is not supposed to be, trying to make up his mind whether to go forward or to turn back. (SOS pp. 69 - 70)

The author's timid use of the language of psychoanalysis is an attempt to anticipate some of the changes the character's psyche must go through if he is to develop a new self. In this very brief moment of intuition brought forth by unintended introspection, the character has an insight which will, later on, prove crucial to him when he strives to bring under control the contradictory forces plaguing the various aspects of his existence. The mirror game has confronted him with the reflection of his unknown self and his appraisal of the disappointing image has revealed to him how necessary it is for him to become a coherent whole. From now on, his efforts to pull his fragmented self together carry a new meaning apprehended soon after by his father's sympathetic "You want to be a whole man, you have to deal with the whole truth." (SOS p. 77) Not surprisingly, Macon's lecture leaves too many questions unanswered and Milkman is even more confused when verbally assaulted by his sister Lena for failing to see a contradiction between protecting their physically weak mother from a violent father on the one hand, and on the other, preventing their sister First Corinthians from "seeing" a man he (Milkman) thinks unfit to marry her. By eventually deciding to date Porter who is said to be "a perfect example of the men her parents had kept her from (and whom she had also kept herself from) all her life ..." (SOS p. 202), First Corinthians is making a most important statement, which the author has her brother fail to understand. After decades of submissiveness and her resulting inability to set her own priorities, she has eventually matured into an independent woman. That Lena proves able to understand quite spontaneously her sister's inner change while Milkman misses the whole point is an indication of the author's desire to remind the reader that women belong to a community of spirit. And like Lena, some of them are fully aware of the conditions imposed on them by their rulers in male dominated society. The long lecture she gives her brother not only sheds light on men's ignorance – as Toni Morrison sees it – of the issue but also clearly brings home the fact that women have to invent their own strategies in order to free themselves from male domination. The truth beyond the whole performance is that women's rights "exist" only to the degree that their rhetorical skills can enable them to talk men into changing for the better. Lena's question "Where do you get the right to decide on our lives?" (p. 217) obliquely underscores the fact that the "unfit" man happens to be of their sister's own choosing. And her answer to her own question leaves no doubt as to what she has in mind: "I'll tell you where. From that hog's gut that hangs down between your legs." (p. 217) This opinion prompted by the author proceeds from an over-reductive perspective on male / female relationships because it overlooks the role women play in keeping the tradition going. It sheds, though, a crucial light on Lena's double awareness that not only did their father do a "commendable" job of mediating the traditional values of patriarchy but also that her brother proves to be a most studious and obsequious receiver of the paternal teachings. In the last analysis, Lena's speech is a rhetorically structured text whose correct interpretation depends on the women's own inference rule. Milkman is perceived here not only as the replica of Macon but, more importantly, as the archetype of the oppressive "other" that needs to be both tamed and educated, for -- as the animalistic imagery seems to imply -- he is dead from the waist up. Lena is not only her brother's keeper, she is also his teacher. Beyond the whole argument, a major statement by Toni Morrison runs through the passage: it is one thing to be sexist, it is another to be aware of it. The fact of the matter is that despite his readiness to side with the weak against the less weak, Milkman fails to see that what he intends to do and what he is taught to do are far apart. He tries to strike a balance between these two poles of attraction but cannot handle the pressure from everybody around him:

> I just know that I want to live my own life. I don't want to be my old man's office boy no more. And as long as I'm in this place I'll be. Unless I have my own money. I have to get out of that house and I don't want to owe anyone when I go. My family is driving me crazy. Daddy wants me to be like him. My mother wants me to think like her and hate my father. Corinthians won't speak to me; Lena wants me out. And Hagar wants me chained to her bed or dead. Everybody wants something from me, (...). Something they think I got. (pp. 223 - 24)

The realization by Milkman that he is all alone has put him in a state of total confusion. The portrait of the character appears now as a dialectic interaction between what he can offer and what the world around him thinks he ought to offer. What his sister and his lover cousin want is for him to stop treating them like invisible entities. Objectively speaking, he can no longer stay in his father's house. To some extent the family has prepared the conditions for his departure from home. All things considered, Milkman – just like most of Toni Morrison's male characters – thinks exclusively of himself in his relationships with women. He does not want Hagar chaining him to her bed yet would be most delighted to have her in his whenever he feels like it. To be sure, at times what he wants is just a woman – any woman at all. The narrator notes ironically that at one point during his epic journey to the South, Milkman "... needed a place to stay, some information, and a woman, not necessary in that order." (p. 268) The right order – from the author's perspective as is implied in the text – becomes apparent when Milkman's remark about the beauty of the women in the village sparks off only suspicion and hostility in the local men. His thoughts are well summed up when the author makes him wonder: "What kind of place was this where a man couldn't even ask for a woman?" (p. 268) The women's issue is here used by Toni Morrison as the starting point of an illuminating analysis of her male characters' psychology. The author has the villagers hate Milkman because he is a threat to their manhood. Everything he either does or fails to do is perceived as an attempt to underrate their masculinity:

> They looked with hatred at the city Negro who could buy a car as if it were a bottle of whiskey because the one he had was broken. And what's more, who had said so in front of them. He hadn't bothered to say his name, nor ask theirs, had called them "them," and would certainly despise their days, which should have been spent harvesting their own crops, instead of waiting around the general store hoping a truck would come looking for mill hands or tobacco pickers in the flatlands that belonged to somebody else. His manner, his clothes were reminders that they had no crops of their own and no land to speak of either. Just vegetable gardens, which the women took care of and chickens and pigs that the children took care of. He was telling them that they weren't men, that they relied on women and children for their food. And that the lint of tobacco in their pants pockets where dollar bills should have been was the measure. That thin shoes and suits with vests and smooth hands were the measure. That eyes that had seen big cities and the inside of airplanes were the measure. They had seen him watching their women and rubbing his fly as he stood on the

steps. They had also seen him lock his car as soon as he got out of it in a place where there couldn't be more than two keys twenty-five miles around. He hadn't found them fit enough or good enough to want to know their names, and believed himself too good to tell them his. They looked at his skin and saw it was as black as theirs, but they knew he had the heart of the white men who came to pick them up in their trucks when they needed anonymous, faceless laborers. (p. 269)

The narrator clearly shows that there is a code of conduct among Blacks in the village. Failure to act it out makes the code violators "white." Or "nigger." The villagers have a set idea what white men are like and Milkman is one of them. Milkman came down South because at some point of his psychological growth he sensed what Susan Willis calls a "loss of history and culture."[38] Aspects of that culture and the history that helped bring it forth are being acted out, here, by some of its authentic custodians. Morrison artistically manages to create a disjunction of the individual from the community and the effort to bridge the gap between the two parties is not as seriously undertaken by them as it is by him. The result is a clash of self-revealing images that inform both the global dimension of the black experience and the many faces of black men. The poor rural South is at odds here with the relatively rich and urbanized North and the covert ideological confrontation both sides engage in puts Milkman at a disadvantage. He is the intruder everybody is accusing without caring how he feels about what he is thought to be. The local men, instead, appear as the victimized heroes whose hospitality, availability, integrity, and manliness are being questioned – or at best, ignored – by someone they originally mistook for a fellow black. Milkman is learning the hard way to move "from selfish and materialistic dilettantism to an understanding of brotherhood."[39] There appears a confusion of issues in the villagers' appraisal of the situation. They are men who are victims of the socio-economic system but blame it on racism by promoting a convenient definition of "blackness" which transcends skin colour and focuses instead on both a state of mind and an attitude of the heart. Milkman is rejected by blacks in the South for the same reason his father was

[38] Susan Willis, "Eruptions of Funk : Historicizing Morrison", in Black American Literary Forum, Vol. 16, Number 1, Spring 1982, p. 35.
[39] Dorothy H. Lee ; "The Quest for Self : Triumph and Failure in the Works of Toni Morrison", in Mari Evans, ed., Black Women Writers (1950 - 1980), Garden city, N.Y., Anchor Press / Doubleday, 1984, p. 353.

once rejected by other blacks in the North. Once again, his decision to control his own life lands him in confusion. But unlike the previous times, Milkman this time around is fully prepared to secure victory over his usual self.

Despite his efforts to detach himself from his father, Milkman is regarded almost by everybody as just Macon's replica. Why he opts for seeking help outside the family circle is easy to understand.

Guitar is clearly Milkman's best friend and it is important to note that Milkman consults him –instead of his own family – on so private an issue as the story behind his (Milkman's) name. The politics of naming as is depicted in Song of Solomon dramatizes both the dehumanizing conditions of existence of the people concerned and the discrepancy between what the latter think they are and what they are perceived as by outsiders. There is no doubt at all that his name plays a very important role in Milkman's life. For one thing, as a young boy he once considered becoming a medical doctor but his conviction that no patient would go see a Dr Dead made him give up the idea. In a community where names tell how little control the people have over their lives, Milkman's quest for the truth about his personal beginnings is a sound foundation for his fast growing willingness to erase up-rootedness from the history of his family. Fortunately, the humanism thus developed by him is constantly nourished by Guitar's availability. Thanks to Guitar, he learns to try harder in life than he used to in his younger years. This does not imply, though, that Milkman is over-influenced by Guitar. What the text suggests, instead, is the commitment of two personalities to growing together and enriching each other. Take for example the discussion on the similarities between the Holocaust and its aftermath on the one hand, and the Blacks Experience in America on the other hand. Milkman's idea that the Jews who hunt down the Nazi criminals do the right thing by bringing their catch to the Courts of Justice is in harmony with his hatred for people who like to take the law into their own hands.

That the author makes Milkman hate any commitment that requires an active involvement or participation on his behalf is borne out by his propensity to run away from whatever problem he does not feel equipped to solve. Even on the unconscious level the character is said to be willing to own only things that have to do with speed and movement. When caught dreaming about what he would do if he could lay his hands on the alleged gold in Pilate's house, Milkman is fantasizing for "boats, cars, airplanes, and the command of a large crew." (p. 180) He wants the money as it can help him flee a past he cannot come to grips with:

> He wanted the money – desperately he believed – but other than making tracks out of the city, far away from Not Doctor Street, and Sonny's Shop, and Mary's place, and Hagar, he could not visualize a life that much different from the one he had. New people. New places. Command. That was what he wanted in his life. (p. 180)

Throughout the novel, the discrepancy is underlined over and over again between the relatively clear representation by Milkman the young adult of his own objective in life and the extremely limited energy he is willing to mobilize to that end.

One of the most important decisions Milkman ever had to make is to go to the South not only for the gold but also for his roots. But the way he anticipates the journey, once again, implies a deep – if unconscious – desire to disappear from this world of ours where he feels utterly helpless:

> The airplane ride exhilarated him, encouraged illusion and a feeling of invulnerability. High above the cloud, heavy yet light, caught in the stillness of speed (...), sitting in intricate metal become glistening bird, it was not possible to believe he had ever made a mistake, or could. (p. 222)

Down here, with his feet on the ground, he is like a bird in a cage whereas up "... in the air, away from life, he felt free ..." (p. 222)

Not only is the journey important but what makes it still more crucial is the fact that for the first time in his life Milkman undertakes something by himself. The Southern epic therefore becomes a series of rites of passage during which the character progressively sheds his old skin in preparation for a new self. The trying spiritual experience even materializes on the physical plane little by little throughout the journey as Milkman loses his belongings, especially his clothes, one after the other. Dispossession is metaphorically depicted by the author as a prerequisite for possession. Milkman symbolically disowns, so to speak, his family in the North in order to join the "tribe" of his other relatives in the South. "He didn't feel close to them, but he did feel connected, as though there was some cord or pulse or information they shared. Back home he had never felt that way, as though he belonged to anyplace or anybody." (p. 296) In one way or another, attention is paid to his inner existence and as a result, he feels connected. Connectedness generates respect and love. It wipes out doubt, brings in the reassuring feeling of belonging. No wonder Milkman, later on, returns to the North as a changed person. In that respect he can be called a winner. The psychological imbalance that used to be constantly part of his life has also disappeared. He no longer sees any point in hating his parents and sisters because now he is a well-balanced person capable of standing on his own feet on the one hand, and adjusting to others, on the other hand. The prospects of a new and healthier relationship with Hagar no longer leave anything to be desired. Unfortunately, the change is untimely. Hagar's sudden death – an irony of fate – is an indication of the necessity for the change to occur as quickly as possible. A man who has always lived up to this principle is Guitar.

1.2.3 Creating a home: Guitar as a political activist

Guitar plays a key role in *Song of Solomon* in the sense that he is depicted by the author as the indispensable link between the hermetic circle of Milkman's family and the rest of the black community. His whole existence is based on the premise that to help fellow blacks regain dignity and self-confidence is a sacred duty that must be taken care of by all means. Unlike Milkman who used to hate his own name, Guitar never bothered himself about his. His perspective on the issue of "slave names" is informed by a philosophy of action structured on the principle that it is far worse being a slave than merely bearing a slave name. His contributions toward the collective evaluation of the meaning of what it feels like to be black in America is all the more important as the alternative the author makes him stand for purports to generate a group dynamics.

Guitar is fully aware that a lot of energy is being wasted on a daily basis by blacks hurting each other. In his view, they all have been fooled into a game they were not appropriately coached to win:

> The cards are stacked against us and just trying to stay in the game, stay alive in the game makes us do funny things. Things we can't help. Things that make us hurt one another. We don't even know why. (SOS p. 88)

Instead of actively seeking to change the rules of the game or learning hard to play it as well as those who initiated it, most blacks Guitar interacts with merely develop a rhetoric that postpones action and purports to promote a semblance of happiness that is experienced on the moment. A case in point is what happened after a group of blacks had discussed the murder in Mississippi by some white youths of Emmet Till who "... had whistled at some white woman, refused to deny he had slept with others, and was a Northerner visiting the South." Not only is no specific decision made as to what could be done in the future to avoid any similar killings but the fact that they did not wind up fighting each other is depicted as a feat in itself. As if to add insult to injury, they end the "meeting" on a funny note:

> The men began to trade tales of atrocities, first stories they had heard, then those they'd witnessed, and finally the things that had happened to themselves. A litany of personal humiliation, outrage, and anger turned sicklelike back to themselves as humor. They laughed, uproariously, about the speed with which they had run, the pose they had assumed, the ruse they had invented to escape or decrease some threat to their manliness, their humanness. (p. 83)

In Guitar's view, the "Nigger Joke" as a way of processing painful experience into folk culture should not be used to delay action in emergency cases. He insists, through his deeds, that he does not believe in this type of coping because it does not eradicate slave status. Guitar's political commitment and the way he expresses it prove right the opinion that "Morrison develops the social and psychological aspects which characterize the lived experience of historical transition."[40] To him, black lives are sacred and the right thing to do is to learn to value them by going to every possible extreme to protect them. Although he is, at times, sensitive to the point of sounding patronizing, he has managed to make hitting back the cornerstone of his political commitment. The aesthetic of the character relies on a conception of "fairness" based on an unquestionable rejection of "coolness". He combats this ability that his people have developed over the centuries to take all kinds of mean racial treatments and let their aggressors get away with it. For nothing to be wrong with blacks controlling themselves, the "other people" (p. 117) also – Guitar re-iterates – must be taught to refrain from killing blacks. He does not believe in mere rhetoric. His race consciousness, as the narrator sees it, proceeds from a Manichean perception of American society which identifies each race as a homogeneous group. The practical result, of course, is that – since unlike

---

40 Susan Willis; " Eruptions of Funk : Historicizing Morrison", in *Black American Literary Forum*, Vol. 16, Number 1, Spring 1982, p. 35.

Milkman he favors fight over flight – he can locate the enemy in every white person he runs into. He holds that all white people are "unnatural." The picture gets even clearer when he dismisses Milkman's point that not all whites are bad. His assumption is that whenever a white-on-black crime is committed, it does not matter who does the killing:

> There are no innocent white people, because every one of them is a potential nigger-killer, if not an actual one ... Milkman, if Kennedy got drunk and bored and was sitting around a potbellied stove in Mississippi, he might join a lynching party just for the hell of it. Under those circumstances his unnaturalness would surface. But I know I wouldn't join one no matter how drunk I was or how bored, and I know you wouldn't either, or any black man I know or ever heard tell of. Ever. In any world, at any time, just get up and go find somebody white to slice up. But they can Do it. (pp. 156 - 57)

Guitar's expression of racial commitment in an ideologically charged language records the individual's assessment, in the light of history, of the group psychology of a whole race. In *Song of Solomon* though, the type of generalization implied by this Manichean stand on the issue of race relationships is used artistically as a most convenient reason by the author to justify anti-racist racism – from Guitar's perspective, that is.

In fact, Guitar does not consider himself racist. To be sure, he does not like white people simply because they remind him of dead people. (p. 60) The fact of the matter actually seems to be that he has transferred onto the white race as a whole his hatred for the white man who used to be his father's employer. He admits to being the way he feels at present ever since he was a kid and more precisely "since my father got sliced up in a saw mill and his boss came by and gave us kids some candy. Divinity. A big sack of divinity. His wife made it special for us." (p. 61) At some other point, he recalls more vividly in a brief moment of introspection not only the full story but more importantly, its implications for his future development:

> And he remembered anew how his mother smiled when the white man handed her the four ten-dollar bills. More than gratitude was showing in her eyes. More than that. Not love, but a willingness to love. Her husband was sliced in half and boxed backward. He had heard the mill men tell how the two halves, not even fitted

together, were placed cut side down, skin side up, in the coffin. Facing each other. Each eye looking deep into its mate... Even so, his mother had smiled and shown that willingness to love the man who was responsible for dividing his father through eternity. It wasn't the divinity from the foreman's wife that made him sick. That came later. It was the fact that instead of life insurance, the saw mill owner gave his mother forty dollars "to tide you and them kids over," and she took it happily and brought each of them a big peppermint stick on the very day of the funeral. Guitar's two sisters and baby brother sucked away at the bone-white and blood-red stick, but Guitar couldn't. He held it in his hand until it stuck there. All day he held it... The others made fun of what they believed was his miserliness, but he could not eat it or throw it away, until finally, in the out-house, he let it fall into the earth's stinking hole. (pp. 226 - 27)

Guitar's bitterness with whites is not based on an abstract speculation. It is sustained, instead, by a concrete experience. The language of trauma being used here by Toni Morrison aims at creating a consolidated memory which generates awareness raising in the character. And awareness raising, in most cases, is a call for action. That the series of events is presented in the form of recollections in the quotation testifies to the impact it has on the person who lived through it. The experience has been processed into permanent bitterness and readiness to fight back.

Yet Guitar, as he is conceived by the author, does not hate whites. He simply does not like them. To him, between not liking white people and hating them, there is enough room for a whole range of ideologies. One such ideology is his membership of the Seven Days. He is delighted to join this activist group which consists of "...a few men who want to take some risks." (p. 155) What comes next is a strong attempt to ethically justify the group's existence:

> They don't initiate anything; they don't even choose. They are as rain. But when a Negro child, Negro woman or Negro man is killed by Whites and nothing is done about it by THEIR law and THEIR courts this society selects a similar victim at random, and they execute him or her in a similar manner if they can. (p. 155)

Milkman's utterance as articulated by Toni Morrison emphasizes the fact that the American legal system is not always on the side of justice. Instead, it tends to be selective in its implementation of the laws of the land and oftentimes blacks are the victims. His mental representation of the black American condition results in a political choice based on a philosophy of violence that uses the end to justify the means. Little wonder the narrator calls Guitar "… a man with blood-deep responsibilities." (p. 181)

Guitar's vision is not limited to his political commitment. His dreams are not about material things that can help him fulfil himself as an individual. On the contrary he wishes he could afford a marker for his father's grave and provide for his (extended) family. In other words, he believes in values dismissed by Macon II as irrelevant. The plight of blacks in general preoccupies him very much but apparently, not as much as that of black men. In an attempt to show Milkman why the black man in America is finding it so difficult to exploit all his potentialities as a person, he relates the particular to the general:

> Look. It's the condition our condition is in. Everybody wants the life of a black man. Everybody. White men want us dead or quiet – which is the same thing as dead. White women, same thing. (…) And black women, they want your whole self. Love, they call it, and understanding. 'Why don't you UNDERSTAND me?' What they mean is, Don't love anything on earth except me. They say 'Be responsible,' but what they mean is Don't go anywhere where I ain't. You try to climb Mount Everest, they will tie up your ropes. Tell them you want to go to the bottom of the sea – just for a look – they will hide your oxygen tank. Or you don't even have to go that far. Buy a horn and say you want to play. Oh, they love the music, but only after you pull eight at the post office. Even if you make it, even if you stubborn and mean and you get to the top of Mount Everest, or you do play and you good, real good – that still ain't enough. You blow your lungs out on the horn and they want what breath you got left to hear about how you love them. They want your full attention. Take a risk and you not for real. That you don't love them. They won't even let you risk your own life, can't even die unless it's about them. (pp. 224 - 5)

One may wonder why Toni Morrison is having Guitar sound so hard on his "sisters." In a previous passage where she briefly assesses the genealogy of black American women's sufferings she had this to say:

> Edging into life from the back door. Becoming. Everybody in the world was in a position to give them orders. White women said "Do this". White children said, "Give me that." White men said, "Come here." Black men said, "Lay down" (The Bluest Eye, p. 109).

In *Song of Solomon*, Guitar is given a chance to respond to this "Lay down". But his response here reads, ironically, like a further indictment of black women. The black man as Guitar is made to see him, perceives the black woman as a permanent threat to his need for self-fulfillment. Her sense of caring is mistaken by him for emotional greed. Her commitment to him is just another strategy of domination he has to keep in check. In any case, the image he has of them indirectly tells what they (black women) perceive black men as. Guitar, as the author sees him, finds them too demanding – emotionally speaking; but such a perception seems to proceed from a misinterpretation of black women's caring about their "brothers". The historical debate between black men and black women as to which of the two groups was the more oppressed in slavery and/or after is swiftly introduced here.

All things considered, the character Guitar symbolizes here what Alice Walker calls "the ignorance of black men about black women." In her opinion, the black woman almost never has to ask of the black man anything he cannot afford to offer her. This is not to say that Morrison would necessarily agree with Alice Walker. The latter's point as indicated earlier on in this study is made most forcefully in her essay "In Search of Our Mother's Gardens". Black women, she emphasizes, want for black men to acknowledge their "labors of fidelity and love" and let them bear fruit. Guitar as Toni Morrison's creation makes no mention of them. Just like Macon Dead, he is portrayed as an over-focused person who has his own priorities and no time to consider other people's feelings.

Oddly enough, Guitar feels that the black woman is his. Assuming that he is not taking black women for granted, one may think that he is planning to improve his relationships with them in the future. He seems to hold that specific problem can "disappear" as soon as the prevailing socio-economic order is revised. His journey to the South is supposed to provide the Seven Days with the funding they need if they are to make their dream come true one day. But the hostility exhibited by Guitar when he thought that Milkman was not willing to share the gold raises questions as to his good faith when he says he values so much black lives. In fact Guitar becomes very suspicious of his former friend probably because the author does not want them connecting psychologically anymore. They no longer belong to a community of spirit and this can be traced to their different political persuasions. That Guitar loses his sanity over the gold is an indication of the kind of psychological instability his "focusedness" can land him in. He appears, however, as a winner because like Macon who has managed to fulfil himself he has achieved, if temporarily, his goal of love through self-denial. His killing Pilate, though by accident, calls for a reassessment of his political commitment. The black men in *Song of Solomon* are not only success-oriented; they also know how to reach their goals. This seems to be the major difference between them and those in *The Bluest Eye* and *Sula*.

The same issues of love, money and the black experience have received a more sophisticated treatment in Tar Baby. Son and the other male characters – no matter what their race – add a new dimension to Toni Morrison's portrayals of black men.

1.3 The divorce from the material: *Tar Baby*

Apart from Guitar in *Song of Solomon*, each of the male characters studied in Toni Morrison's novels assessed in the context of this study has a woman in his life. None of the above mentioned women has ever accepted her man's account of himself. In their everyday lives, the women in Toni Morrison's fiction expose the reality of a situation whereby the discrepancy between what men think of themselves and what women perceive them as, highlights the power that men have and what use they put it to. As far as the representation of black men goes, the originality of *Tar Baby* in the work of its author lies in the contrast between Son the man, and Jade the woman he is made to team up with. In contrast to what we discover in *Song of Solomon*, where despite their higher education the Dead girls are not career-oriented, *Tar Baby* brings together a man with very little formal education and a highly ambitious professional woman. No wonder it appears to Darwin T. Turner that "when one compares *Tar Baby* with Morrison's earlier works, Jadine and Son seem too ordinary, too stereotypical – created solely to demonstrate the clash of class and culture."[41] The novel records the implications of Son's goal in life and how this goal affects psychologically his relationship with people around him.

Tar Baby is set on a small Caribbean island called L'Arbre de la Croix where Valerian Street, a retired white industrialist, turns their summer residence into a definitive home against the will of his wife Margaret. They share their home with their two black servants, Ondine and Sidney Childs, who have been married for several decades but have no children. Valerian sponsored the education of Ondine's niece Jadine (Jade in short) both in America and in France, where she studied art and modeling.

When food starts disappearing from the basement the butler Sidney first blames it all on rats. One night, though, Margaret, who hardly gets along with her husband, retires to her room only to find a black man with dreadlocked hair sitting in her closet. "She stood in the doorway screaming, first at Valerian and then at Jadine, who rushed to her side." (p. 78) Before allowing Son into the picture, the author makes sure that Margaret is perceived by the reader as a frail person incapable of defending herself. Her helplessness is further stressed as "She (...) balled her beautiful hands into fists and pummeled her own temples, screaming louder." (p. 78) This white woman who is a romantic combination of frailty and beauty proves unable to name what she just discovered in her closet, and when she eventually manages to whisper "Black" – with "her eyes shut tight," (p. 79) – nobody understands her. Many a woman, under similar circumstances, would have said "A man" or "A black man." When scrutinized against the background of the dramatic irony exhibited by the omniscient narrator in the presentation of the conversation (pp. 78 - 9), Margaret's choice of word reads like an affirmation of her whitness – a whiteness she feels is threatened. Surprisingly enough, while Margaret is struggling to recover from the shock, Valerian makes sure that the intruder is treated as a member of the household. As a matter of fact Valerian's reception of Son takes everybody by surprise: "Good evening, sir. Would you care for a drink?" Apparently Toni Morrison is about creating a very liberal white man. By having this unexpected reaction, Valerian expresses the type of attitude he would like to have toward the intruder. Margaret's fear, in the author's description, is counterbalanced by her husband's self-confidence. By allowing the stranger to stay in the house Valerian has created the necessary space where important actions are to take place in the future. For one thing, the coming together of the black man and

---

41 Darwin T. Turner; "Theme, Characterization, and Style in the works of Toni Morrison", in Mari Evans, ed., *Black Women Writers* (1950 - 1980), Garden City, N. Y., Anchor Press/Doubleday, 1984, p. 369.

Jadine is made easier thanks to the landlord's move. It takes the newcomer long to reveal his identity: at first all we know is that he calls himself Son, is originally from the West Indies, and lived in the United States for many years.

In terms of the representation of males, *Tar Baby*, more than any other novels by Toni Morrison studied here is fraught with pluri-faceted characters whose various images are the constructs of the consciousnesses around them. Soon after Son is discovered in the house and is asked to stay – to be consequently waited upon by a reluctant Sidney –the latter overhears a conversation between his wife and the stranger in the kitchen. He steps in and the long argument that takes place between the two men is most revealing:

> "What are you doing in my place?" Ondine held up a hand. "He came to apologize, Sidney." Son moved aside so he would not be standing between them and said, "Yes, Sir …" "anything you got to say to me or to my wife, you say it somewhere else. You are not invited in here." "It was Jadine," Son began. "She suggested…" "Jadine can't invite you in here, only I can do that. And let me tell you something now. If this was my house, you would have a bullet in your head. Right there." And he pointed to a spot between Son's eyebrows. "You can tell it's not my house because you are still standing upright. But this here is." He pointed a finger at the floor. "Mr Childs, you have to understand me. I was surprised as anybody when he asked me to stay -" Sidney interrupted him again. "You have been lurking around here for days, and a suit and a haircut don't change that." "I'm not trying to change it. I'm trying to explain it. I was in some trouble and I left my ship. I couldn't just knock on the door." "Don't hand me that mess. Save it for people who don't know better. You know what I'm talking about, you was upstairs!" "I was wrong, okay? I'm guilty of being hungry and I'm guilty of being stupid, but nothing else. He knows that. Your boss knows that, why don't you know it? "Because you are not stupid and Mr Street don't know anything about you. White folks play with Negroes. It entertained *him*, that's all, inviting you to dinner. He don't give a damn what it does to anybody else. You think he cares about his wife? That you scared his wife? If it entertained him, he'd *hand* her to you!" "Sidney!" Ondine was frowning. "It's true!" (Sidney insists) "You know him all this time and you think that?"

she asked him. "You tell me," he answered. "You ever see him worry over her?" Ondine did not answer. "No. You don't. And he don't worry over us neither. What he wants is for people to do what he says do. Well, it may be his house but I live here too and I don't want *you* around!" Sidney turned back to Son, pointing at him again. "Mr Childs," Son spoke softly but clearly, "you don't have to be worried over me either." "But I am. You the kind of man that does worry me. You had a job, you chucked it. You got in some trouble, you say, so you just run off. You hide, you live in secret, underground, surface when you caught. I know you, but you don't know me. I am a Phil - a - delphia Negro mentioned in the book of the very same name. My people owned drugstores and taught school while yours were still cutting their faces open so as to tell one of you from the other. And if you looking to live off the fat of the land, and if you think I'm going to wait on you, think twice! He'll lose interest in you faster than you can blink. You already got about all you can out of this place: a suit and some new shoes. Don't get another idea in your head." "I'm leaving, Mr Childs. He said he'll help me get a visa – something – so I can get back home. So…" You don't need no visa to go home. You a citizen, ain't you?" "Well, I use another name. I mean I don't want nobody checking me out." "Take my advice. Clean your life up." (pp. 162 - 3)

This passage dramatizes three male images. The authoritarian Sidney Childs, who is seeking to take over from his employer Valerian Street in order to deal with Son properly, occupies a strategic position in the narrator's technique of exposition. The author establishes the character's authority by emphasizing two facts. He is black and he has been working for – and living with – a white man for quite a long time. He therefore feels qualified to articulate what Valerian and Son are about. Even Ondine is not allowed to question her husband's claim. The irony of the situation is that the part of the house he wants to keep Son away from is the kitchen. Hunger forced Son into the house. So, he needs the kitchen, if only metaphorically. Sidney's intention to symbolically starve the stranger finds expression in his threat to Son's life. Because Sidney regards himself as an authority on both black and white issues he needs no explanation from a fellow black to understand the latter's motives. The colorful language in which the author has him dismiss Son's own reasons for being in the house both underlines Sidney's self-proclaimed position as the ultimate custodian of the truth and obliquely conveys Valerian's ignorance about blacks.

As the conversation moves on, Morrison creates two contradictory images of Valerian, with each of the two black men trying to promote one. Evidently, Son is judging Valerian as an individual and on the basis of a specific, punctual decision about him, whereas Sidney sees his boss just as the representative of a whole race. "White folks play with Negroes," he says. The other irony is that the more Son tells Sidney about himself, the more convinced Sidney is of knowing the intruder's nature. Sidney, in the narrator's view, regards himself as an expert on human nature. He can read people's souls and tell whatever they are about although he remains a secret to them: "I know you but you don't know me." And he holds both the power and the authority that legitimate his knowledge as a birthright. He is a Philadelphia Negro, i. e. one of the "emancipated" career-oriented blacks whose "case" was studied by W. E. B. Dubois in his famous book *The Philadelphia Negro*. Being from that class alone – as Toni Morrison ironically has the character believe – is a sign of cleverness and, as a result, no explanation from Son can ever convince him of the good faith of the stranger. As a matter of fact, one may understandably suggest that after drilling certain ideas into his boss about blacks, Sidney is afraid that Son might promote another "black" image that could affect Sidney's life around Valerian.

From Son's perspective, Valerian Street is caring and understanding, and the record of his actions suggests on his behalf a fairly liberal stand on racial issues. But as a Philadelphia Negro who knows better, Sidney suggests that on account of Valerian's race, the latter belongs to a fixed category of people. The Manichean world promoted by Guitar in *Song of Solomon* is, once again, anticipated. Once the basic idea is posited that whites play with blacks, the butler's next move is to account for his boss's current difference as far as treating a stranger as a human being is concerned. It may be true that Valerian derives pleasure from inviting Son to dinner but his character as seen by Sidney consistently appears sustained by a self-centeredness that affects even Valerian's married life. He cares about nobody but himself. Ondine's "you know him all this time and you think that?" raises a lot of questions about the accuracy of her husband's view of Valerian. She uses the observation to set the record straight. Her contribution consequently underlines the importance of a feminine input whose function in the definition of the "object" under depiction consists not only in balancing out a masculine position but most of all in humanizing the image eventually obtained. It is this humanized image of Valerian in his relationship with blacks that prevails until he decides to fire Gideon, the yardman.

The meaning of Valerian Street in *Tar Baby* is crucial to the understanding of most of the other characters in the novel. He owns a mansion and employs many people. Those are well-known symbols of wealth, and in Morrison's fiction wealth has always been depicted as a metaphor for power: Valerian is an achiever who, by virtue of what he owns, has a lot of power at his disposition. Ironically enough, he is not often allowed by the author to use that power. Unlike the authoritarian Macon Dead II, in *Song of Solomon*, who dictates to every person that depends on him, the only person Valerian can successfully "push around" is his wife. Valerian's authority is very often undermined, if not openly questioned, by his employees. To some extent, the first time he actually uses his power is when he fires Gideon and, unsurprisingly, his decision sparks off only hostility around him. Gideon's dismissal is a turning point in the depiction of Valerian's character. By having the yardman fired by his boss for stealing a few apples, the author creates a circumstance that forces Son – among other characters – to reassess his perception of his benefactor. That a man of Valerian's wealth could take such an action against a poor worker is beyond Son's understanding.

The representation of this rich, liberal white is the first full length portrayal of a white male by Toni Morrison in her early fiction. The techniques used by the author to depict him include both letting the character's actions speak for themselves and allowing, at the same time, blacks from his entourage to generate a discourse that aims to underline the impact of white presence on their everyday lives. While in a novel like W. W. Brown's *Clotel* there is no discrepancy – roughly speaking – between the way white men act and what their black observers have to say about them, in *Tar Baby*, by contrast, there is an overt sense of commitment to re-evaluating old, received ideas in light of new experiences. In this respect, one can see many striking similarities between the ways both Valerian and Son are represented.

Son is said to be "a man without human rites..." and what follows is an incomplete list of those deficiencies: unbaptized, uncircumcised, unmarried, undivorced, propertyless, homeless, etc. Once again, the black man in Morrison's fiction is posited in terms of what he is not or what he lacks. Now those rites are extremely important in the sense that they alone can provide any individual with the appropriate psychological strength that it takes to feel a regular member of any community of human beings. A human being without any rites is, in actual fact, entitled to no rights, and Son confirms this by joining, for the first eight years of his life in America, "that great underclass of undocumented men." Throughout his early American years, Son is depicted as a non-entity. Oddly enough, his realization of his "ritelessness" does not lead him to face his helplessness. He does not surrender to the fact that he is excluded from society; instead the author makes him creatively transform what should be regarded as a handicap into a source of power that can sustain him in the expression of his difference. In his opinion, something is wrong with rites. And he has always wanted "another way." Such a choice clearly conflicts with many previous representations of black men, especially in the fiction of black male writers. In Ralph Ellison, Richard Wright, James Baldwin and many others, black men overtly wish to experience the "human rites" in order to qualify to fit into American society.

When the author eventually decides to have Son's "real" self emerge as she imagines it, at first it shows itself in his repeated use of a certain four letter word. His consistent use of this language – a semantically charged representation of what he thinks about her – provokes revulsion in her later on when he decides to talk to her in a more direct way. The Sorbonne graduate quickly notices the difference in their backgrounds and the response she receives ("Goddam") to her question "Don't you have any other word to express awe?" (p. 117) confirms her fear. What she does not realize, though, is how disconnected Son feels from her and whatever she stands for. This gap is progressively bridged. The first stage is Son's insinuation that for Jade to be so successful a model in Europe, she has to have been a prostitute in the Old World:

> Jadine jumped away from the desk and leaned forward trying to kill him with her fists while her mind raced to places in the room where there might be a poker or a vase or a sharp pair of shears. He turned his head a little but did not raise his arms to protect himself. All he had to do was what he did: stand up and let his height put his face and head out of her easy reach. She stretched nonetheless trying to tear the whites from his eyes. He caught both her wrists and crossed them in front of her face. She spit full in his face but the saliva fell on the C of his pajama top. Her gold-thread slippers were no good for kicking — but she kicked anyhow. He uncrossed her wrists and swung her around, holding her from behind in the vise of his arms. His chin was in her hair. (pp. 120 - 1)

This image of the black man who stands tall and cool in front – metaphorically – of the threat represented by the black woman is even taken one step further. Son does not strike back. Instead, the final scene of the segment ("His chin was in her hair") suggests a romantic involvement initiated by the man. By meeting female adversity with male love the author presents Son not as an enemy any more but rather as a potential friend and/or a protector of Jade. The new situation generates only frustration in Jadine because the fight he has just started is actually meant to provide the appropriate outlet to her anger. No wonder that she misreads Son's loving gesture. "You rape me and they will feed you to the alligators. Count on it, nigger." (p. 121) Whatever the reason behind this misreading, the message has the merit of bringing up, once again, the worn out stereotypical image of the black man as a rapist. It seems important to note here that there exists an important scholarship by an increasing number of black women which tends to insist that rape becomes an issue only if the victim is white. The point is made time and again by Trudier Harris[42] and Paula Giddings,[43] to cite just two examples. Read against such a background, Son's response "Why you little white girls always think somebody's trying to rape you?" (p. 121) is more than ironical. By assuming in his question that all rapists are black and that all rape victims are white, the author clearly questions Jade's "blackness" and puts Son in the position of an arrogant man who thinks he knows what it takes to be a black woman. For some time now, black women have been consistently denying black men the right to define black womanhood. The way they see it, for a black man to claim that he can tell a black woman what she is or ought to be instead of just contributing a male input toward black women's self definition is to treat black women like immature children. However, Jade acts defensive enough for the reader to assume that she doubts her own blackness. As Trudier Harris puts it: "Through education, severing of connection to black people, and general disposition, Jadine is "white". She has traded a cultural heritage for what she considers the finer things of life ..."[44] The second stage of Jadine's anger as imagined by the author is therefore provoked by what she regards as Son's insult.

---

42 *Exorcising Blackness*, Bloogmington, Indiana University Press, 1984.
43 *When and Where I Enter*, New York, W. Morrow, 1984.
44 Trudier Harris, *Exorcising Blackness*, 1984, p. 153.

Despite this aggressiveness openly expressed by both parties, Son and Jade are pulled together by external forces. It is a fact that Son's coming to L'Arbre de la Croix caused Valerian's household to split into many factions. Only Valerian himself "liked" the intruder right from the beginning. And yet as time passes by, Jade becomes sensitive to what Son is perceived as. When Margaret at the very beginning dare not call him "nigger", evidently because she thinks Jade might take offence at the word, the latter swiftly makes her white friend feel comfortable calling a spade a spade. Later on, though, when Margaret says Son looks like a gorilla, a sudden change occurs in the black woman: "Jadine's neck prickled at the description. She had volunteered nigger – but not gorilla." (p. 129) Toni Morrison is putting in the same category of whites Margaret and the bargeman in *Sula* who recovered Chicken Little's body from the water. They both see blacks as animals. To their conception Morrison opposes Jade's outlook. From the foregoing example and many more, one may conclude that throughout *Tar Baby* the character Son – or more precisely the representation of him – functions as a literary device used by the author to hold the various episodes of the story together. His very presence in the house has generated between the members of the household a dialectics that has not left himself unchanged. In the description of Son's psychological condition from the moment he jumps ship to when he gets caught in Margaret's room, a recurrent motif is his preoccupation with everything but women. Over and over again, the point is made that "He had not followed the women." But after sleeping for a few nights in Margaret's room a change starts taking place in him.

The beginning of Son's romantic involvement with Jadine offers the author another opportunity to elaborate more on Son's personal beliefs and attitudes which are clearly articulated in his life story. The narration is basically made by the character himself and Jadine's contribution consists of questions that her interlocutor cannot evade. As was suggested earlier on, everyone Son interacts with has his or her own mental representation of him. One consequence, therefore, of Son's "confession" to Jade is that her new image of him is informed by knowledge no other person in Valerian's house has access to. She is closer than anybody else to the center that holds the various images of Son together because she knows the "truth". And the truth is that he is a murderer on the run. He killed by accident his unfaithful girlfriend and her teenage lover. And after narrating such a story, he simply proceeds to tell her "I won't kill you. I love you." (p. 177)

But Morrison makes sure his love has some difficulty growing. The first major crisis takes place when Valerian fires two of his house-servant – Gideon the gardener and his wife Therese – for stealing his apples. Not only is the news broken while the "family" is having a large Christmas meal but in addition Jadine unexpectedly sides with her old "patron" against the unfortunate two:

> Valerian at the head of his Christmas table, looked at the four black people; all but one he knew extremely well, all but one, and even that one was in his debt. Across from him at the bottom of the table sat Son who thought he knew them all very well too, except one and that one was escaping out of his hands, and that one was doing the bidding of her boss and "patron." Keeping the dinner going smoothly, quietly chastising everybody including her own uncle and aunt, soothing Margaret, agreeing with Valerian and calling Gideon Yardman and never taking the trouble to know his name and never calling his own name out loud. He looked at Valerian and Valerian looked back. The evening eyes met those of the man with the savannas in his face. The man who respected industry looked over a gulf at the man who prized fraternity. (pp. 204 - 5)

A similarity is created by the author between Sidney and Valerian. Just as Sidney claims that he knows white folks as well as black people, so is Valerian portrayed as somebody knowledgeable about the people in his house. At the same time, his hospitable treatment of Son, in retrospect, is presented as a callously calculated strategy destined to cripple Son psychologically. Even the locations of Valerian and Son facing each other at the Christmas dinner table convey the sense that Valerian is in the stronger position. By creating a gap between the two men on the one hand and on the other hand, by making one cherish industry and the other one fraternity, the author once again creates focused characters and seems to imply that they cannot reach out and touch each other. Their first attempt to do that was, understandably, short-lived. Once the deceiving liberal appearance at first exhibited by Valerian is shattered by his own deeds (seen mostly from Son's perspective), he becomes vulnerable to somebody like Son who has been waiting for the first opportunity to strike. When he does strike, the presentation of the two men's states of mind is made in a more expressive way as soon as they start talking to each other. In fact, when Son does verbally attack his host, the resulting ideological confrontation between the boss and the intruder clearly indicates that they do not belong together.

The expression by Son of his difference triggers off the rest of the action. The situation is very well summed-up during the argument in Valerian's utterance: "I am being questioned by these people as if I could be called into question!" (p. 208) The author is having Valerian verbalize what everyone knew all along: he owns everything and provides for everyone in his house. He respects industry and should be respected for that. Valerian's is the voice of the dominant culture and, thanks to the shift of voice, Morrison insists that he does not think it necessary for him to respect poor people. All things considered, Gideon becomes an important part of the narrative only when he is no longer in the picture – physically speaking. And the task of opening people's eyes to the gardener's importance has been assigned to Son. The latter knows for a fact that by Valerian's standards only people who own things are important and respectable. To reverse the trend, as Son is made to see it, is to define the terms of a new dialogue between the haves and the have-nots. The notion of fraternity which, at first, suggests the coming together of the exploited poor in general quickly fades into something similar to the Black Brotherhood in Ralph Ellison's *Invisible Man*. Most of the issues he raises force Valerian to make sure that he (Valerian) keeps in control in his own house. The rhetoric they both engage in aims, in the case of Valerian, to maintain unchallenged the power he knows he has whereas in the case of Son it aims to dismantle the very foundation of that power. Viewed against this background, Ondine's rebellion against her employer becomes the artistic expression of Son's influence. He wishes Jadine also were influenced by him. Unfortunately, all he can remember her doing throughout the whole debate is "…watching her pour *his* wine, listening to her take his part, trying to calm Ondine and Sidney to *his* satisfaction." All things considered, Jadine to him looks just like a replica of Valerian. But in addition to whatever she has in common with her "patron", she is perceived by the author – at this stage of the story – to be weak and incapable of standing on her own feet.

Son has internalized the basic principles of the male culture he was born into and which taught him – among other things – to be protective of women. In a moment of introspection he therefore assesses his duty to Jadine in light of his interpretation of that culture:

> (U)nderneath her efficiency and know - it - all sass were wind chimes. Nine rectangles of crystal, rainbowed in the light. Fragile pieces of glass tinkling as long as the breeze was gentle. But in more vigorous weather the thread that held it together would snap. So it

would be his duty to keep the climate mild for her, to hold back with his hand if need be thunder, drought and all manner of winterkill, and he would blow with his lips a gentle enough breeze for her to tinkle in. The bird-like defenselessness he had loved while she slept and saw when she took his hand on the stairs was his to protect.

This rhetoric of female frailty that needs a male presence to lean against does not draw any clear-cut distinctions between the physical, the emotional, and the psychological. It therefore makes too many demands on Son. If he is to guarantee Jade every kind of protection, he has to make sure first of all that he himself is psychologically stable. And he is not. The narrator's evaluation of the internal turmoil experienced by the character is illuminating to that effect:

> For if he loved and lost this woman whose sleeping face was the limits his eyes could safely behold and whose wakened face threw him into confusion, he would sure lose the world. So he made himself disgusting to her. Insulted and offended her. (p. 220)

The anger which originates from the realization of the dilemma is not expressed openly. It explains, though, Son's temporary decision to stop functioning from the heart as far as his relationship with her goes. But he feels incapable of hating her, which is why he tries to have her hate him instead. He prefers to give her "... sufficient cause to help him keep his love in chains..." (p. 220)

Their life as a couple in America is another background against which another dimension of Son's character is portrayed. There is ample evidence in the novel that, in Son's view, to help Jadine is to help her rebel against whatever Valerian stands for. Son's desire to have Jadine unlearn what it took her a whole lifetime to learn proceeds from a philosophy of education that focuses the cultivation of respect for the individual for what he/she is and not for what he/she owns. His refusal to join the ratrace is referred to by her as "ignorance." (p. 264) Jadine, as is reiterated throughout the novel, has learned "to make it in *this* world." (p. 264) Her insistence on the importance of the material and Son's point that "I don't want to *make* it. I want to *be* it." (p. 266) are unfortunately presented as two strictly defined and unalterable alternatives. The debate between the two lovers sheds some light on the philosophical interpretation of the Afro-American cultural heritage as the tar-baby story in the novel suggests. From Jadine's perspective, to stick to the black cultural tradition is to "stay in that medieval slave basket..." (p. 271) whereas for Son, joining mainstream American society is a nightmare. Their final break-up initiated by Jade takes place as a result of her inability to change or manipulate Son. All things considered, Son's divorce from the material did not win him a stable relationship with Jadine because he was not equipped with the appropriate psychological strength that could have enabled him to meet her halfway by accepting that one can strike a balance between making it and being it – whatever "being it" means. In that respect, his final decision to join her in L'Arbre de la Croix in order to give their love a second chance is simply a belated loss of innocence. By delaying Son's psychological maturation the author has succeeded in making him realize retrospectively that he gave up a woman he loves simply "(b)ecause she had a temper, energy, ideas of her own and fought back." (p. 298)

As was earlier on emphasized in this chapter, money plays an important role in Toni Morrison's fiction. It generates a power that is easily processed into the language spoken by the rich to define what they want and what they think the dispossessed need. Her male characters, when wealthy like Macon Dead and Valerian Street, become the center that holds together the shattered lives of many others and the respect that comes with their very existence is perceived by them as their ultimate objective in life. At the same time, though, the quest – among blacks – for material wealth invariably takes place in the context of cultural dispossession. This "fact" probably accounts for Son's commitment to "being" it as opposed to "making" it. In one way or another, Morrison's black men are depicted as going through a painful process of culture change. Ironically enough, she consistently defines them in terms of what they do not know, or cannot do, what they are not or what they may not offer. They are therefore confronted with the dominant culture as potential losers. By contrast, Morrison's black women are defined in terms of what they can do or produce. In their relationships with black men, their ability to manipulate and silence their husbands has no limit. Unsurprisingly, the male have-nots are at the mercy of situations and events beyond their control. They find the pressure of (married) life extremely hard to handle and cope by running away from the women in their lives - like Boyboy, Cholly, Jade, and Son - only to realize that they cannot even afford to be on their own, which is why they run to other women. The black men who choose, mainly for ideological reasons, not to believe in money become social outcasts or a threat to mainstream American society. What all these men have in common, though, is a certain inability to go quickly beyond their own conceptions in order to come to grips with the complexity of the human reality that they are part of.

2

ALICE WALKER'S BLACK MEN

ALICE WALKER'S BLACK MEN

In the first part of this study I tried to show how in her depiction of black men Toni Morrison emphasizes the psychological handicap from which they suffer. By contrast, in Alice Walker's *The Third Life of Grange Copeland*, *Meridian* and *The Color Purple* there seems to be a shift of emphasis. Admittedly she depicts in all her writings the confusion black men experience whenever they are confronted with the moving reality of their lives. Unlike Toni Morrison who sets most of her early fiction in the North and dwells, in the process of depicting black men, on the psychological disintegration most of them experience, Alice Walker sets her three novels under consideration here in the South where the impact of the prevailing social structure on the black individual is much stronger. As far as the depiction of black men goes, Alice Walker seems to pick up where Toni Morrison leaves off. Walker places a special emphasis on the black man's "marginal" attempts to both assert his manhood and meet his needs as a human being.

2.1 Manhood Redefined: A Study of Alice Walker's *The Third Life of Grange Copeland*

In her essay "Zora Neale Hurston: A Cautionary Tale and A Partisan View,"[45] Alice Walker makes the point that "racial health is the quality she feels is most characteristic of Zora's work..." And this notion as she understands it is simply "a sense of black people as complete, complex, undiminished human beings..."[46] To a large extent Alice Walker's work is a repeated effort

---

45 Alice Walker *In Search of Our Mother's Garden* (pp. 83 - 92)
46 Ibid. p. 85

to make sure that her spiritual mother's message is heard and understood by men and women of all races. As a matter of fact, her first novel[47] *The Third Life of Grange Copeland* sheds a crucial light on a world where black women learn progressively to stop functioning as diminished presences. Even when posited as diminished presences, black women in Alice Walker's early fiction are still perceived as potential troublemakers by black male characters who consequently seek to wrap them in silence. But not all black women in *The Third Life of Grange Copeland* are shut down for good. Walker emphasizes that those of them who try – and manage – to assert themselves expose in the process *the mentalities* of the black men who want them erased. In this chapter I will take a close look at the male figures in these relationships.

Brownfield Copeland, Grange Copeland's only child, grows up on a plantation in Georgia and realizes in his early adulthood that "his own life was becoming a repetition of his father's." (p. 54) The combination, by the author, of this painful memory of the past and the possibility that it might mortgage the future, brings together the lives of three generations of Copelands, because Brownfield's statement is uttered in the context of his realization that his oldest child, Daphne has now become "the lone little pickaninny" (p. 54) on his boss's cotton plantation. Throughout the first half of the novel, Grange is portrayed as a virtual slave. The author has him stay in the South, in contrast with his brother Silas. By keeping Grange in the South, the author creates the conditions for a realistic comparison between two socio-economic orders. The first step towards the realization of this "project" becomes apparent when Brownfield's cousins "told him that their own daddy, his uncle Silas had gone to Philadelphia to be his own boss." (p. 5)

At this stage of the narrative, the implied author tells Brownfield where to draw the line between his own father Grange and his uncle Silas. Grange is not a risk taker; Silas is. This insinuation only prolongs the manipulation of the mood of the story in which the author engages at the very beginning of the novel by making Brownfield look worthy of the reader's empathy. From Bromfield's perspective, Grange exists only as the opposite of Silas. The latter knows how to go for good and nice things in the North whereas the former is not good at causing things to happen in his own life. The image he has internalized of his father is what his cousins visiting from Philadelphia had told him years before. "They told him that his father worked for a cracker and

---

[47] *The Third Life of Grange Copeland*, New York : Harcourt Brace Jovanovich, 1970. All subsequent quotations are from this edition.

that the cracker owned him." (p. 4) That this crucial information is provided by outsiders whom the author posits as innocent is a clear indication of the silence Bromfield has to cope with in the circle of his immediate family. Slave status as has been experienced by Grange is a series of attitudes drilled into him by white society and which prevent him from living as a self-determined person. The abundant sociological description of the human environment where Grange lives in Georgia underlines the little control he has over his own life and those of the people depending on him. His manhood is affected in such a way the very fact that he manages to survive at all is portrayed as a feat in itself.

As a virtual slave, Grange knows that he is not even entitled to the right to protect his family because even in the privacy of his married life, Shipley his "owner" is the ultimate boss. Grange's wife Margaret is quick to realize this: after only two years of marriage she knew that in her plantation world the mother was second in command, the father having no command at all. Grange also has a first-hand experience of what it feels like to be confronted with the reality of Margaret's finding:

> "Grange, save me! Grange help me!" she had cried the first time she had been taken by the first in command. He had plugged his ears with whiskey, telling himself as he ignored her, that he was not to be blamed for his wife's unforgivable sin. He had blamed Margaret and he had blamed Shipley, all the Shipleys in the world. (p. 178)

In the author's presentation, the black woman is seen as a cheap piece of property by the white man and from the fact that Alice Walker does not make Grange challenge Shipley's authority it seems obvious that she means to establish a tacit understanding between the two men as to what each of them is about. Grange remains a virtual slave because Shipley is a virtual slaveholder. As Bertram Karon observes:

> Whatever the Negro's difficulty may be in shifting from thinking of himself as an inferior being to thinking of himself as an equal, the blocks are much greater for the white man who must shift from thinking of a piece of property to thinking about a human being with the self-same property he reserved to himself. The white man has never fully made the shift, but merely made various

compromises between treating (and thinking of) the Negro as a slave and as an equal.[48]

Grange's inability to function as a husband who can provide his wife with the protection she needs is at first presented by the author as a result of the imbalance between the two opposing forces. The way he chooses to resolve the situation, though, tells the story of his maladjustment. Only when drunk can he convince himself of his wife's unforgivable sin. Instead of having him reflect on his plight in order to devise ways of getting closer to his wife within the limited space where they both are allowed to function, the author chooses to make him blame his wife for not defending herself. In the final analysis, although it is Shipley who sleeps with Grange's wife against her will, it is Grange who is portrayed – indirectly – as the rapist.

Bromfield's sympathy goes to his mother instead. For one thing, "he blamed his father for his mother's change." (p. 20) The manipulation of the mood by the omniscient narrator, once again, can be traced to the concern of a female observer who is more than willing to "justify" what Margaret herself believed to be sinful. In the narrator's words: "… it was Grange she followed at first. It was Grange who led her to the rituals of song and dance and drink (…). It was Grange who had first turned to someone else." (p. 20) The social structure of which Grange is a part is ill adapted to the needs he feels as an individual. His marriage no longer offers him any opportunities for the fulfillment of the goals of social life as defined by the whole community. He reacts the way he knows how. Unsurprisingly, Grange's unfaithfulness to his wife leads the latter to follow suit by engaging in the bad behaviors listed by the author.

> And even when Margaret found relief from her cares in the arms of her fellow bait-pullers and church members, or with the man who drove the truck and who turned her husband to stone, there was a deference in her eyes that spoke of her love for Grange. On weekdays when sober and wifely, she struggled to make food out of plants that grew wild and game caught solely in traps, she was submissive still. It was on weekends only that she became a huntress of soft touches, gentle voices and sex without the arguments over the constant and compelling pressures of everyday life. She had

---

48 Bertram P. Karon, *The Negro Personality*, New York: Springer Publishing Company, Inc., 1958, p. 10.

sincerely regretted the baby. And now, humbly respecting her husband's feelings, she ignored it.

Grange survives his wife who "had died believing what she had done was sinful and required death, and that what he had done required nothing but what she get out of his life." (p. 178) By making Margaret take to the grave the secret of her own ignorance, the author allows the dead woman to shed a special light on Grange's previous life. He lives to regret his past mistakes. If he now "thought with tears in his eyes what a fool he had been" (p. 178), it is not so much because of those past deeds as it is because of the possibility that they might happen to other people in the future.

A father is supposed to be a role model to his sons; now until his son Bromfield gets married, Grange Copeland's life has been a series of humiliations and exhibitions of his powerlessness. No wonder that he has never had anything to tell his son as the latter grows up. As a father, Grange fails to provide a basis from which Brownfield could later on operate as an adult. Growing up with a father who "almost never spoke to him unless they had company," (p. 5) Brownfield Copeland spends his childhood listening to "the familiar silence around him." (p. 5) What he cannot hear his father say, he tries to see him do. He soon establishes that Mr. Shipley, the white man whose plantation his father has been working on all his life, terrorizes Grange by his sheer presence:

> Brownfield's father had no smiles about him at all. He merely froze; his movements when he had to move to place sacks on the truck were rigid as a machine's. At first Brownfield thought his father was turned to stone by the truck itself. The truck was big and noisy and coldly, militarily gray. Its big wheels flattened the cotton stalks and made deep ruts in the soft dirt of the field. But after watching the loading of the truck for several weeks he realized it was the man who drove the truck who caused his father to don a mask that was more impenetrable than his usual silence. Brownfield looked closely at the man and made a startling discovery; the man was a man, but entirely different from his own father. (p. 8)

All his married life, as Alice Walker imagines it, Grange has symbolized psycho-social maladjustment. Even from the young Brownfield's perspective he does not live up to the "norm." He is only his father whereas the white man, "the man", has something more about him. He is an index of manhood by the standard of the dominant culture. In other words, if "the man" is a man but at the same time entirely different from the man that Grange Copeland is, the difference obviously symbolized by Mr. Shipley's whiteness is the space where the narrator sees fully authorized manhood standing tall next to unauthorized and therefore crippled manhood. In the case of Grange's relationship with his wife Margaret, the white man has not been processed into a castrating presence, as happened to Cholly Breedlove in Toni Morrison's *The Bluest Eye*, when he was caught by two white males in the bush in the company of his first girlfriend. In either case, though, the anger aroused in the black male is directed against the black women. Although *The Third Life of Copeland* has only few white characters in it, almost every episode of the narrative tells the story of the white man's power over the Southern sharecroppers' lives. To be sure, this power is often over-valued by the black men, which is why one can admit that "… Brownfield uses white racism as an excuse for his moral decay."[49] The Copelands live in the environment where violence is experienced on a daily basis:

> Their life followed a kind of cycle that depended almost totally on Grange's moods. On Monday, suffering from a hangover and the aftereffects of a violent quarrel with his wife the night before, Grange was morose, sullen, reserved, deeply in pain under the hot early morning sun. Margaret was tense and exceedingly nervous. Brownfield moved about the house like a mouse. On Tuesday, Grange was merely quiet. His wife and son began to relax. On Wednesday as the day stretched out and the cotton rows stretched out even longer, Grange muttered and sighed. He sat outside in the night air longer before going to bed; he would speak of moving away, of going north. He might try to figure out how much he owed the man who owned the fields. The man who drove the truck and who owned the shack they occupied. But these activities depressed him, and he said things on Wednesday nights that made his wife cry. By Thursday, Grange's gloominess reached its peak he grimaced respectfully, with veiled eyes, at the jokes told by the

---

[49] Klauss Ensslen : "Collective Experience and Individual Responsibility : Alice Walker's *The Third Life of Grange Copeland*" in Peter Bruck and Wolfgang Karrer, eds. *The Afro-American Novel* since 1960, 1982, p. 206

man who drove the truck. On Thursday nights he stalked the house from the room and pulled himself up and swung from the rafters of the porch. Brownfield could hear his joints creaking against the sounds of the porch, for the whole porch shook when his father swung. By Friday Grange was so stupefied with the work and the sun he wanted nothing but rest the next two days before it started all over again.

On Saturday afternoon Grange shaved, bathed, put on clean overalls and a shirt and took the wagon into town to buy groceries. While he was away his wife washed and straightened her hair. She dressed up and sat, all shining and pretty, in the open door, hoping anxiously for visitors who never came.

Brownfield too was washed and cleanly dressed. He played contentedly in the silent woods and in the clearing. Late Saturday night Grange would come home lurching drunk, threatening to kill his wife and Brownfield, stumbling and shooting off his shotgun. He threatened Margaret and she ran and hid in the woods with Brownfield huddled at her feet. Then Grange would roll out the door and in the yard, crying like a child in big wrenching sobs and rubbing his whole head in the dirt. He would lie there until Sunday morning, when the chickens pecked around him, and the dog sniffed at him and neither his wife nor Brownfield went near him. (pp. 11 - 12)

The weekly scenario of Grange's life is the cycle that the novel seeks to replicate. As the life of the family depends on Grange's moods, so does the spiral along which the story evolves. The various images of his married life projected by the author from different perspectives underline Grange's inability to mobilize the energies that can help him face his responsibility as both a father and a husband. His repeated threat to kill Brownfield and Margaret is the ultimate result of his psycho-social maladjustment. Grange generates around him much more sufferings than he is made to endure.

Brownfield has picked up where his father left off. The irony of the situation is that he has always wanted to be different. By the time Brownfield realizes that his own life has been progressing along a path previously traveled by his father, he is already married with one daughter. Like his father, he first of all blames most of his problems on the person closest to him: his wife Mem. Not surprisingly, in the depiction of Brownfield as a villain in his father's image, the female sensitivity once again prevails. The dialectics of his mistreatment of Mem is captured by the author in a series of commentaries. Brownfield decides that having married Mem is a "mistake" (p. 55), starts beating her on a regular basis, and refuses to take full responsibility for his own failure. He has become a monster who cannot fit anymore:

> The tender woman he married he set out to destroy. And before he destroyed her he was determined to change her. And change her he did. He was her Pygmalion in reverse. The first thing he started on was her speech. They had begun their marriage with her correcting him, but after a very short while this began to wear on him. He could not stand to be belittled at home after coming from a job that required him to respond to all orders from a stooped position. *When she kindly replaced an "is" for an "are" he threw her correction in her face.* (My emphasis)

This short passage is pregnant with many potential consequences some of which need to be elaborated upon here. According to George Steiner (quoted by Henry Louis Gates, Jr. in his Figures in Black; p. 172): "... the human being performs an act of translation, in the full sense of the word, when receiving a speech-message from any other human being. Time, disparities in outlook, and distance make this translation even more difficult." The character Mem as imagined by Alice Walker has some formal education, which both socially and psychologically speaking places here, if only symbolically above her husband Brownfield. She is equipped to read into the setting of their common narrative values he does not believe in. In that context one easily understands the discrepancy between what Mem says to him and whatever he takes her to mean.

One should keep in mind that Mem is a school teacher by profession. According to M. A. K. Halliday "... it is the teachers who exert the most influence on the social environment. They do so not by manipulating the social structure [...] but by playing a major part in the process whereby a human being becomes a social man."[50]

---

50 M. A. K. *Halliday Language as Social Semiotic*, p. 9

Therefore while seeking to change Brownfield's syntax, Mem actually has a hidden agenda which consists in teaching his husband to progressively learn to play new social roles and achieve social mobility at the end of the day. "It is by means of language that the 'human being' becomes one of a group of 'people' [...]; by virtue of his participation in a group the individual is no longer simply a biological specimen of humanity – he is a person."[51] There is every indication in the narrative that Brownfield is not willing to change "groups" or become "a person." He seems to like it where he now is. And not only that. He also wishes to bring Mem *down* to his level, and teach her *his* language.

Thus, Brownfield's intention as conceived by the author is not only to destroy his "tender" wife physically but also psychologically. By forcing her to learn to account for the reality of her inner world by means of a "borrowed" tongue—the only one Brownfield understands—he expresses a strong desire to disfigure her soul. In the narrator's estimation, his ultimate goal is to make her sound like "... a hopeless nigger woman (...) who deserves him." (p. 56) The implication that Brownfield himself is a "nigger", i. e. a failure, is soon written is bold characters when the author makes the reader see him in the company of his peers. While they admire how much alcohol he can drink and wonder how he managed to marry a woman of Mem's class, he reminds them of another dimension of his achievement: "'Give this old black snake to her,' he said, rubbing himself indecently, exposing his life to the streets, 'and then I beats her ass. Only way to treat a nigger woman!'" (p. 56) This segment reminds one of the passages in Song of Solomon, where Toni Morrison has Lena reduce her brother Milkman to his penis. In Alice Walker, though, it is the black man who consciously promotes the self-defeating phallocentric account of himself. The character's self-perception and the omniscient narrator's perception of him coincide, which makes Brownfield's married life read like the record book of people's failure to adjust themselves to a society on the move. Brownfield's character is conceived as a unique chance given Grange to scrutinize the replay of his own life. The similarities are striking. The one big difference seems to be the crucial role played by Mem in bringing Grange to full maturity – not that he quickly takes the opportunity offered by his wife to make himself a better person.

---

51 Ibidem. P. 14

Brownfield has spent all his life trying to erase his wife. In the couple's joint projects as they are depicted by the author, he proves inconsiderate and in fact does not even remember that he is party to a deal. At first he spends on a pig the money they were saving together to buy a house. In many cultures and civilizations the house stands for stability and rootedness. And most psychologically balanced people love having one. When Mem decides to go it alone this time, Brownfield is once again in the way. He uses the money of the second attempt "for the down payment on a little red car." (p. 57) Only he can understand his own priorities. His wife's endeavors to move out of the sharecropper's world are annihilated by him. He does not even wonder whether there are some ways out. To be sure, Alice Walker had her marry him out of love but he was in his teens. Despite his young age, the author soon makes him sense that he will have to depend on himself for the solutions to his various problems. The pressure from life on the plantation is manipulated in order not to leave his family life unaffected. So the author makes sure that the popularly acknowledged pattern fully applies to him. He assumes that his wife Mem was "being used by white men, his oppressors, a charge she tearfully and truthfully denied. And when he took her in his drunkenness and in the midst of his own foul accusations, she wilted and accepted him in total passivity and blankness, like a church." (p. 54) When jealousy in him is sustained by a sense of worthlessness, sex becomes the only means Brownfield can think of to convince himself that he is still in control. In so doing, he reminds the reader of Grange's younger years when his motto used to be "if I can never own nothing, (...), I will have women." (p. 177)

The disintegration of the character into the type of black male that Eldridge Cleaver, in *Soul on Ice*, calls the "Supermasculine Menial," actually begins the very day Brownfield marries Mem. As in Toni Morrison's *Tar Baby* where the education of Jadine is primarily perceived by Son as a threat in an eventual relationship, Mem's "knowledge reflected badly on a husband who could scarcely read and write." (p. 55) The character Brownfield as shaped by Alice Walker is petrified by a strong black woman like Mem. The strategy that the author uses to have him beak his wife is to cause him to drag her away from school-teaching. But obviously, it is not enough preventing her from professionally expressing her "superiority" on a daily basis. To help "his crushed pride" and "his battered ego" recover from the situation, he makes the decision "to bring her down to his level" (p. 55) by sending her into white homes as a domestic. This way of looking at "equality" is in fact a camouflaged attempt to pattern his lifestyle in a manner that brings him closer to Mr. Shipley. Mem is made to pay the price for her husband's symbolic ascension because for the power that he now has to be real, he has to exercise it over real people and see how it works.

A most brutal expression of the newly acquired power takes place when Brownfield learns that his wife is not willing to move with her family to J. L.'s, a place owned by Captain Davis, the new man Brownfield now has to work for. The fact of the matter is that Mem prefers to get a house in town in order to better their daughter's chance of getting good education. Brownfield takes offense because not only does she not want to move to another plantation but in addition she wants to move to another place of her own choosing. As a matter of fact, two conflicting visions of the future are at war here. While Brownfield is unconsciously favoring the perpetual reproduction of the cycle of violence -- poverty and maladjustment-- the author is having Mem see literacy and education as a means to break it. During the argument that they have upon her return from town, he passes a new rule: "I ought to make you call me Mister,' he said, slowly twisting the wrist he held and bringing her to her knees besides his feet. 'A woman as black and ugly as you ought to call a man Mister." (p. 77) The image of a black woman kneeling down at the black man's feet is the materialization of the master-slave relationship Brownfield has always wanted to have with his wife. It is revealing to know that, in the author's perception, the moment Mem is in a weak and defenseless position her blackness is equated with ugliness by the husband who is supposed to protect her.

When, days later, Brownfield in a new attempt to display his authority, thunders: "we going to move over on Mr. J. L.'s place," his wife uncompromisingly fires back: "I ain't, and these children ain't." (p. 52) For the first time ever, Mem has the courage to assert herself by saying NO to her husband. This moment of the narrative is extremely important. As a matter of fact, both characters are placed in the same setting and exposed, by the author, to the same realities permeating the said setting. However, Mem and Brownfield do not feel the same ways about the same realities. Actually, Mem's NO results from an analysis, by her, of the master discourse represented (and produced) here by Brownfield. Mem, this time around, has the courage to tell her husband how she *feels* about their *common realities* and she uses language to communicate to him her difference. She is for change and the new language she uses is meant to be a vector of it.

Prior to this crucial event, Mem was depicted as a shadow of Brownfield. He used to think that he molded her and shaped her; in other words, he dutifully sought to delete her as an individual entity -- 'a person'-- by structuring around her a silence similar to the one he had to live through as a child. Mem who has been ignored all her married life has just opted for not ignoring back. She acknowledges him as a person by demanding that he break away from his usual self. Brownfield's old self is deeply rooted in a passive acceptance of the sociological conditions prevailing in the plantation world. As long as his definition of manhood is informed by that frame of mind, he will be denying himself and his daughters the chance to take the various opportunities that America has to offer. As a matter of fact, she intentionally let him don the mask of head of the family for a long time but to no avail; looking back now she realizes that her "decision to let him be a man of the house for nine years had cost her and him nine years of unrelenting misery." (p. 86)

Alice Walker sees a striking similarity between the black man-black woman relationship and the white man-black man relationship. Mem's and Brownfield's problem is just the microcosm of a more general situation. Her NO therefore, is the meeting point of the old and the new. The old is the resignation philosophy drilled into blacks both in slavery and after, which teaches them to blame it all on each other or on the white man, whereas the new holds that the possibility exists for them to creatively manipulate the prevailing situation to their own advantage by tapping into a noble part of themselves.

Although Grange is late in realizing that a NO like Mem's is crucial to the survival of his people in America, he deserves a lot of credit for making it a new starting point as he engages in rethinking manhood. No wonder that when his new wife Josie complains to Grange that not only did Brownfield fail to have a father in childhood but to top it off now "the white folks was just pushing him down in the mud," (p. 206) he takes the opportunity to lecture Josie, his granddaughter Ruth, and Brownfield on what manhood is all about:

> You see, I figured he could blame a good part of his life on me; I didn't offer him no directions and, he thought, no love. But when he becomes a man himself, with his own opportunity to righten the wrong I done him by being good to his own children, he had a chance to become a real man, a daddy in his own right. That was the time he should have just forgot about what I done to him – and

to his ma. But he messed up with his children, his wife and his home, and never yet blamed himself. And never blaming hisself done made him weak. He no longer have to think beyond me and the white folks to get to the root of all his problems. Damn, if thinking like that ain't made noodles out of his brains. (p. 206)

In this scene the author-narrator brings together three generations of Copelands and the statement is uttered in the context of a family feud. This opportunity is used by the author to fuse the past and the present into a meaningful set of ideas that will sustain a bright future for the new generation. Grange acknowledges that he has already failed twice in the sense that his son's life so far has been a replica of his own. Somebody has to break the cycle. By making Ruth a witness to the performance, the author makes her part of the new beginning. She is the reason why Grange can afford to live for the third time. In this respect, Barbara Christian is fully right to hold that *"The Third Life of Grange Copeland* (...) is based on the principle that social change is invariably linked to personal change, that the struggle must be inner - as well as outer-directed."[52]

The idea that never blaming oneself makes one weak is central to the writing of most black American feminist novelists. In that respect, Zora Neale Hurton's *Their Eyes Were Watching God* can be regarded as the starting point of a new tradition in the post Harlem Renaissance era. In that tradition, many female characters eventually mature into assertive and self-determined women who show their newly acquired inner force by conquering male-conceived speech. What they have to say whenever they have access to man's language disturbs the foundation of the whole structure upon which lies men's power. That power has been protected through violent means for generations, which is the secret Mem has discovered living with her husband in *The Third Life of Grange Copeland*. When she decides to terrorize Brownfield with the gun he starts behaving exactly the way he had wanted her to behave when he was "in power". As long as she was behaving the way he thought fit, Brownfield did not need to engage in an introspection that could have led him to blaming himself.

To go back to Grange. To be sure, his refusal to undermine people's accountability for their own actions or plight puts an end to a long tradition of

---

[52] Barbara Christian: "Alice Walker: the Black Woman Artist as Wayward" in Mari Evans, ed., *Black Women Writers* (1950 - 1980) Garden City, N.Y., anchor Press/Doubleday, 1984, p. 460.

women blaming it all on men or blacks holding whites totally responsible for their poor condition. The irony, though, is that it took him a third chance for him to correct some of the mistakes he made in his younger years.

The crucial family reunion is used by the narrator as the beginning of a new era in the narrative itself. The rest of the story is told, in fact, through the consciousness of Ruth, especially when it is her grandfather talking, reflecting or acting. Using his belated maturity as a yardstick, he tries to convey the impression that unlike his son, he is no longer a whiner. By taking full responsibility for preparing Ruth to face life with determination and self-confidence while, at the same time he is "against her acting boyish," (p. 214) Grange and, lurking closely behind him, the author, are promoting a new womanhood based on femininity without dependence. The breed of women that the new Ruth now represents calls for a new breed of men if they are to survive. In that respect, one understands why Grange "became softer than Ruth had ever known him." (p. 207) In Grange's newly conceived world, girls get tough without going boyish whereas men become soft without turning effeminate. Fair enough. But Grange's theory and its implementation as articulated by the author have a few inconsistencies to them. While it is clear that the grandfather is committed to preparing his granddaughter to protect her "purity and open-eyedness and humor and compassion …," (p. 214) the ambiguity of Alice Walker's style in the next statement is an indication of some sort of confusion: "Assured, by his own life, that America would kill her innocence and eventually put out the two big eyes that searched for the seed of truth in everything, he must make her unhesitant to leave it." (p. 214) In my opinion, it is not clear what Ruth must leave. Should it be America, her symbolic alienation from mainstream American culture will simply result in a further isolation of blacks in the new world.

Some of the inconsistencies in Grange's new outlook can be traced to the fact that its definition of the new manhood is not a fully conceived philosophy of action but simply a series of occasional declarations of intent. It is also revealing that whenever Grange has something important to say in relation to the necessity for change in the black American community, he talks in the presence of Ruth. This way of assigning the new black woman a relatively active role in the redeeming process underlines the urge to start off a collective action although the focus seems to be on individual decisions. The profile of the new man is therefore informed by an awareness that being one's own positive person in a hostile environment can bear all the more fruit as the individual proves able to come to terms with a whole range of contradictions. Take for example this following statement:

> I know the danger of putting all the blame on somebody else for the mess you make out of your life. I fell into the trap myself! And I'm bound to believe that that's the way the white folks can corrupt you even when you done held up before. 'Cause when they got you thinking that they're to blame for everything they have you thinking they's some kind of gods! You can't do nothing wrong without them being behind it. You git just as weak as water, no feeling of doing nothing yourself. Then you begins to think up evil and begins to destroy everybody around you, and you blames it on the crackers. Shit! Nobody's as powerful as we make them out to be. We got our own souls, don't we? (p. 207)

Swiftly, Grange is blaming something on "the white folks" here. But the dialectics of the conversation brings the precision of meaning and the delineation of content. Being a man is diving deep inside oneself for the appropriate psychological resources which can harden the individual in front of the worst adversity and make him retain his faith in – and commitment to – whoever trusts him, depends on him and/or loves him. In view of the general context of the novel, it implies unconditional love and total dedication to one's people. It is a victory over oneself. The past, therefore, must be critically evaluated in the present for the future to be worth living for. The constant presence of the past in the present is even reiterated when the narrator depicts the new Grange poring over Ruth's bible:

> He had great admiration for the Hebrew children who fled from Egypt land. For perhaps the hundredth time he told Ruth the story of the Hebrew exodus.
> "They done the right thing," he said.
> "Did they?"
> "Got out while they still had some sense and cared what happened to they spirit. Also to one 'nother. I may be wrong, but nothing ain't proved it yet." He looked thoughtfully over the book at the fire.
> "What ?" asked Ruth.
> "We can't live here free and easy and at home. We going crazy."

"Here?"

"I don't mean this farm; I mean in this country, the U.S. I believe we got to leave this place if we 'spect to survive. All this struggle to keep human where for years nobody knowed what human was but you. It's killing us. Thye's more ways to git rid of people than with guns. We make good songs and asylum cases."

Maybe it would be better if something happened to change everything; made everything equal; made us fel at home," said Ruth.

"They can't undo what they done and we can't forget it or forgive."

Is it so hard to forgive 'em if they don't do bad things no more?"

"I honestly don't believe they can stop," said Grange, "not as a group anyhow."

(pp. 209 - 210)

The mood being set in this dramatization of the Copelands' uncertainty about their future obliquely announces the Civil Rights Movement of the 60's as the deus ex machina which will make their hopes worth entertaining. This part of the story leaves Brownfield uninvolved. In his own way, he has always sensed, if vaguely, that it takes a lot of dedication and self-denial to find one's way in the world he lives in. All his life Brownfield has tried to do just that. But he also knows from experience that parenting could be a lot easier for him to handle had he had his father's attention as a child. Viewed from that perspective, Grange's rhetoric sounds like an a posteriori justification of his own failure to be a real father – and a man – when Brownfield gave him the chance to. To some extent Grange's point holds that no matter how much pressure is exerted on a black man by both the people and the socio-economic structure of America *"you got to hold tight a place in you where they can't come."* Then again, this is mere abstract speculation to Brownfield, who has never been taught where the man is to be found inside every male.

Grange, as the narrator reiterates over and again, is committed to the idea that once the relationships between black men and their "sisters" have improved, the children resulting from their union will find it very easy to take the trip within themselves and come up fully prepared to face life as healthy people. And those children could grow up as whole human beings and become the sound foundation upon which a better future for the community could be built.

Unlike Brownfield, Grange acknowledges the historical and unconditional commitment of most black women to black men as well as the negative response so many of them receive form their "brothers." He unequivocally blames this state of affair on black men – to the utter disappointment of his son: "we guilty, Brownfield, and neither one of us is going to move a step in the right direction until we admit it." (p. 209) Brownfield is not about admitting "a damn thing" to his father. Not only is he loaded with socio-economic problems which do not give him the time to engage in philosophizing like his father, but in addition his strategy for survival excludes admitting to a crime against any black woman, especially the one he married. To confess to any such guilt is to strip himself of his manhood. He killed his wife in the name of it. To some extent, he sues his father for Ruth in the name of the same pride. Ironically enough, his efforts were perceived differently by his daughter. The grandfather and the granddaughter are agreed that only Brownfield stands for the eternal reproduction of a very dangerous cycle. Brownfield's murder by his own father eventually breaks the cycle and provides Ruth with a new range of alternatives.

As much as Grange hates black on black violence, he is also fully aware that "the gun is very important" for the simple reason that "I don't know that love works on everybody." The paradoxical nature of the double warning contained in these propositions testify to the hesitations of a mind in the making. To recommend, as he does, " a little love, a little buckshot" (p. 196), as a way for Ruth to handle herself when he is no longer there to protect her is to indirectly encourage the further disintegration of the black family. Apparently, though, he sees things differently for the time being. The last years of his life are an illustration of his strategic combination. If he can get emotional and cry along with Ruth at the thought that he could lose his granddaughter to Brownfield, he is also able to gun down his own son just to get him out of his way. As Trudier Harris observes, "Brownfield was the monster he created, and Brownfield is the monster he decided to destroy. (…) His recognition of this two-way responsibility completes his philosophical position."[53]

Ruth is portrayed as a cause worth living and fighting for. She embodies a chance of self-creation enhanced by women's input. This chance of self-creation is simultaneously initiated by men and women whose evaluation of their own life history validates their choice for a radical internal change. Her life is sustained by the support system of her grandfather's ideas. Viewed from

---

53 In R. Baxter Miller, ed. Black American Literature and humanism, p. 65.

that perspective, Grange lives on within his granddaughter. The black woman, in this context, is made the custodian of a most important legacy.

The two main black men in *The Third Life of Grange Copeland* are made to spend the greater parts of their lives trying to cope as individuals. In the process of surviving, the author involves them in irresponsible practices that undermine the future as well as the well-being of the people close to them. As a result, social rites and symbols no longer carry any weight to them. They live on the margins of mainstream society. Two generations of women died from their men's inability to transcend their everyday difficulties in order to live as psychologically balanced individuals. To a large extent, the portrayal of the character Brownfield as a replica of his father Grange, is an attempt by Alice Walker to illustrate in her own way the stereotypical image of the black man as a helplessly victimized person totally incapable of handling the impact of the structure of slave society under the supervision of the white man in the American South. Grange Copeland's comeback is, therefore, a successful attempt to break the stereotype and by the same token to indicate some ways out of the vicious circle. With the death of the two Copelands, the past seems buried for good. The only survivor is Ruth, the embodiment of the ideas of the older Grange. The message she carries illuminates parts of the lives of the characters of *Meridian*.

2.2 The Black man in an inter-racial relationship: An approach to *Meridian*

The *Third Life of Grange Copeland* dramatizes black women's wish for a new breed of men willing to give male-female relationships a new chance. The type of black man that Alice Walker is promoting in her first novel is no longer crippled by the pressure exerted on him by the dominant culture. Instead, he lets his conscience be his only judge and, once rid of all the complexes and the anger which used to plague him, he allows his new self to come into being. As a result of this rebirth, he looks at American reality in a new light.

In *Meridian*, the Civil Rights Movement – in so far as one may look at it as a revolution of mentalities – points the way to a better understanding between blacks and whites by focusing on the interrelatedness of the needs as well as the interests of both communities. It is against the background of this relatively improved and healthy atmosphere that the character Truman Held is depicted in an interracial love relationship with Lynne Rabinowitz, an exchange student on a fact-finding mission from the North.

The novel is set in the South and deals essentially with the personal growth of Meridian, a black woman who, at some point, was in love with Truman Held, the handsome civil rights activist. It was Meridian who first introduced Truman to Lynne and then lost him to her. In the opening chapter called the "last return," which in fact closes the narrative, the author focuses on Chicokema, a Southern town with a tank:

> It had been brought during the sixties when the townspeople who were white felt under attack from "outsider agitations" – those members of the black community who thought equal rights for all should be extended to blacks.

The image of the formerly divided city as is drawn here by Alice Walker announces the author as a politically committed observer of life in the South. Chicokema is a place of contradictions. The author depicts it as a town where conflicting factions have to come to grips with their hostility towards each other in order for them to live in a semblance of harmony. It is a place where the worst thing that can happen to anyone is to be poor. In the words of Meridian's mother: "The answer to everything (…) is we live in America and we're not rich." (p. 56) This way of representing being American and poor as an awful combination, because of the pain that comes with it for the individual concerned or for the community at large, reminds the reader of many other cases in Meridian where the whole consist of (two) conflicting parts. The author sees Truman Held as a black/man, Meridian as a black/woman, Lynne as a white/woman who wishes to be treated as a Jewish/woman.

The novel presents interracial dating as an activity not many people engage in down South. Not that people are not drawn to each other across the race line; they are. In spite of its strict sexual morality (as is depicted in the episode where the body of Merilene Oshay the unfaithful wife killed by her husband is displayed) the South has to live with many other contradictions. The character Truman fully testifies to black men's attraction to white women. On purpose, it seems, the author goes beyond this "fact" and recalls to memory the other combination: despite the prevailing philosophical attitudes held by most Southern whites, the fact of the matter is that white men have always been attracted to black women. "Some of them liked black women for sex and said so. For the others it was a matter of gaining experience, initiation into the adult world. The maid, the cook, a stray child, anything not too old or repulsive would do." (p.107) The author's hostile voice seems to indicate that love is excluded from these white man-black woman relationships, which is a way of reducing her white men to what, in *The Third Life of Grange Copeland*, Brownfield sees himself as a sign of. Only Brownfield has no power at all next to a white man. The author's portrayal of white men as very powerful individuals is highlighted by the fact of Henry Oshay's freedom. Everybody approved of what he did when he killed his adulterous wife. In addition, he has been making money off the dead body for years without any voice ever being raised against him.

It is obvious in the author's view that the power structure sustaining many white men's authority makes most black women easy preys for them. The painful stories of rape which black women keep telling their daughters seem to be part of a defense strategy that purports to educate the younger generation. When Mrs. Hill, Meridian's mother, tells her daughter about how, as a maid, she was often harassed by her boss's son, a twenty-one-year-old kid who could have been her grandson, the feeling aroused in her is plain disgust. This disgust later on is processed into "weary religion - restrained hatred." And it is with this sentiment that she described white men. Mrs. Hill's perception of white men is achieved through an artistic combination of both her personal life story and the collective evaluation, by black people, of their several-century-long existence in the New Continent. This evaluation Amiri Baraka, in another context, called the "emotional history"[54] of black people in America. Although it does inform in Alice Walker's fiction all black Americans' representation of America and, as a result, their interaction with whites, the evidence seems to indicate that every generation scrutinizes it from a farther perspective than the previous generation. Details which carry a lot of weight to one group may be overlooked by another. If Meridian remembers almost everything her mother told her about white men, she remembers almost nothing of what her mother told her about white women. Whatever the reason or reasons behind her selective memory, it is used by Alice Walker as an excuse to have Meridian's personal impression of white women complemented by her grandmother's certainty about them. Not surprisingly, Meridian and her grandmother hold a number of similar views on the subject. They both tend to think white women "frivolous, helpless creatures, lazy and without ingenuity." (p. 108) But the difference between them both is just as important as the similarities. Unlike her grandmother who is afraid of the white woman as a "baby machine"

---

54 Amiri Baraka, *Home*, New York, Morrow, 1966.

because "all the little white people" produced by her are seen by the black woman as potential oppressors, Meridian does not entertain such a fear. In addition, she doesn't even see white girls as potential rivals when it comes to dating black men. Her confidence proceeds quite naturally from what she was taught as a child: "nobody wanted white girls except their empty-headed, effeminate counterparts –white boys." (p. 108) The character Truman Held is the living proof that not many black men share this view.

Against such a psycho-social background, a mixed couple appears necessarily as an oddity. The fact of the matter is that in Alice Walker's Meridian the black man and the white woman belong each to a different tradition in which, as far as selecting a spouse goes, there exists a code of conduct that advises them against choosing a partner from the "other" group. The two codes of conduct may be sustained by two different sets of reasons but the truth of the matter is that they are implemented to the same end. To love, let alone marry, across the race line is, therefore, to degenerate into a code violator.

The character Truman Held is presented, right from the beginning, not only as a man committed to the Civil Rights Movement but also as a product of Meridian's fantasies. When he and Meridian first meet and before one can tell what he thinks and why, his physical appearance is already assessed from Meridian's perspective:

> She could not help staring at his nose, which was high-bridged and keen and seemed to have come straight off the faces of Ethiopian Warriors, whose photographs she had seen. It was wonderfully noble, he was dressed in blue jeans and a polo shirt and his shirt front was covered with buttons. That he wore lots of buttons struck Meridian as odd, too playful, for such a cool, serious man. She wanted buttons like that, though. (p. 81)

This idealized image of Truman turned into a noble Ethiopian warrior dressed in Western attire tells the story of Meridian's fantasies as imagined by the author-narrator. Truman seems to be the reflection of something that wants to come out from deep inside Meridian's soul while at the same time she makes an obvious effort to identify with the picture that she sees of him. Truman's commitment to the cause of the movement is so total he does not even notice her infatuation with him. Ironically enough, the emotional discrepancy between them is not allowed to work against the political harmony that lies at the basis of their involvement in the movement. Truman's dedication to the black cause, at times, is confusingly expressed in the shape of a personal interest in Meridian.

If Truman's looks have not changed, Meridian's perception of him has, over the first year of their friendship. Looking back, the narrator gives a sketchy account of her change and its consequences:

> Everyone thought him handsome because his nose was so keen and his skin was tan and not black; and Meridian, though disliking herself for it, thought him handsome for exactly those reasons, too. Or had, until, when she had known him for about a year, she began to look closely at him. With scrutiny, much of the handsomeness disappeared behind the vain, pretentious person Truman was. And his teeth were far from good. (p. 99)

The author has pronounced the Ethiopian warrior dead in Truman and what remains of him is just a 'regular' black man. As Meridian's excitement wears out, her appreciation of physical beauty changes and tends to depend on her evaluation of the inner person behind the mask of physical appearance. By the time Meridian uncovers the "vain, pretentious person Truman was" (p. 99) behind the handsomeness of his tan skinned Ethiopian figure, she has gone too far to pull back. By throwing "open the door for him" with passionate force, Meridian gives herself the chance to see and feel what still closer scrutiny can reveal about him. That they are not interested in the same thing becomes obvious first of all from the linguistic gap he creates between them by constantly speaking French to her. When eventually he decides to go back to their common English language, the gap is ominously maintained. Little wonder that the night Meridian and he were supposed to go to a party together Truman suggested that they stay home because "... we'll be alone. I want you;" to which Meridian responds: "I love you." (p. 109) The narrator's warning that "... the sly, serious double takes were still in the future" (p. 99) is an attempt by the author to pull the bits and pieces of Truman's current behavior patterns together and, in the process, give us a glimpse of what is to happen next.

Lynne Rabinowitz appears in the picture as the center of "a gigantic flower with revolving human petals." (p. 129) This romanticized depiction of a white woman with her hair being combed by a group of happy black children in a circle around her marks the beginning of a new life for Truman. The children "might be bridesmaids preparing Lynne for marriage. They do not see him. He frames a picture with his camera but something stops him before he presses the shutter. What stops him he will not, for the moment, have to acknowledge: it is a sinking, hopeless feeling about opposites, and what they do to each other." (p. 129) Whether the opposites here are Black and White, man and woman, or black male and white female, Truman's coming together with Lynne is already anticipated and his instant attraction to her proceeds from the "hopeless feeling." The chaos of racism and mutual hatred has consistently prevented blacks and whites from getting to know each other, which explains why after several centuries of co-existence in America they still find each other exotic. The view the author seems to be expressing here is that placing too much emphasis on the differences between people is a way of negating their common ground. In the case of Lynne and Truman the evaluation of the differences is done within the broader framework of the Civil Rights Movement as a social revolution. Anybody involved in this revolution is supposed to get rid of their old selves in preparation for a new common future. Truman is no exception to the rule. It is striking, however, that with Meridian he would make no concession whereas with Lynne he can afford to be flexible:

> Truman had had enough of the Movement and the South. But not Lynne. Mississippi – after the disappearance of the three Civil Rights workers in 1964 – began to beckon her. For two years she thought of nothing else: If Mississippi is the worst place in America for black people, it stood to reason, she thought, that the Art that was their lives would flourish best there. Truman, who had given up his earlier ambition to live permanently in France, wryly considered Mississippi a just alternative. And so a little over two years after the bodies – battered beyond recognition, except for the colors: two white, one black – of Cheney, Goodman and Schwerner were found hidden in a backwoods Neshoba County, Mississippi, dam, Lynne and Truman arrived (p. 130).

Lynne has a clear idea what she wants to do with her life. Her decision to discover the black experience in its various manifestations constitutes the backbone of her personal commitment. Truman, therefore, appears in the picture as the expression of Lynne's consciousness. By letting him give up "wryly" his life dream in order to become the shadow of Lynne in the process of fulfilling herself, the author has created a vacuum in Truman.

When scrutinized against the background of Truman's own perspectives on interracial unions at one point of his personal growth, this daring act of love and self denial represents a big change in the character. When, ignoring Meridian's love for him he first dated the exchange student ² for many months, it is not clear whether he did it out of love or just for the sake of it. Judging from the emotional and intellectual shock he experienced reading W. E. Dubois's *The Soul of Black Folk*, after the white girls had gone back to the North, he sounds truly infatuated with the encounter. " 'The man was a genius!' he cried, and he read the passages from the book that he said were reflective of his and Meridian's souls." (p. 106) Whatever passages are read to Meridian are open to speculation. In the context of the sixties where all of a sudden "BLACK" became beautiful because it could serve all kinds of political purposes, one key passage could well be where Du Bois is teaching his brothers and sisters to learn to derive pride from blackness.[55] Whatever the case, unless Truman's statement is meant to be a strategy used by him to win back Meridian's love or friendship, one may wonder why "He was startled by the coolness with which she received his assertion that what he had decided, after reading "*le maître*," was that if he dated white girls it must be, essentially, a matter of sex." (p. 106)

In his new relationship with Meridian, Truman reveals more aspects of his intimate self which are conveyed in the text through Meridian's consciousness. Meridian, who was first married to one Eddie and bore him a child, is fully aware that she used to lack courage, initiative and a mind of her own. Black history saves her by providing outstanding models whose lives she could

---

55 « After the Egyptian and Indian, the Greek and Roman, the Teuton and Mongolian, the Negro is a sort of seventh son, born with a veil, and gifted with second-sight in the American world,-- a world which yields him no self-consciousness, but only lets him see himself through the revelation of the other world. It is a peculiar sensation, this double-consciousness, this sense of always looking at one's self through the eyes of others, of measuring one's soul by the tape of a world that looks on in amused contempt and pity. One ever feels his twoness, -- an American, a Negro; two souls, two thoughts, two unreconciled strivings; two warring ideals in one dark body, whose dogged strength keeps it from being torn asunder.
The history of the American Negro is the history of this strife,-- this longing to attain self-conscious manhood, to merge his double soul into a better and truer self. In this merging he wishes neither of the older selves to be lost. He would not africanize America, for America has too much to teach the world and Africa. He would not bleach his Negro soul in a flood of white Americanism, for he knows that the Negro blood has a message for the world. "W.E.B. Dubois, *The Souls of Black Folk*, Greenwich, Conn., Fawcett Publications, Inc. (1903), 1961, pp. 16 - 17.

pattern her own after. One such model is "Harriet Truman, the only American woman who'd led troops in battle." This is certainly good for Meridian, who has every reason to try to become an exceptionally strong fighter, i. e. the exact type of black woman Grange has managed to bring forth in The Third Life of Grange Copeland. "But Truman, alas, did not want a general beside him. He did not want a woman who tried, however encumbered by guilts and fears and remorse, to claim her own life. She knew Truman would have liked her better as she had been as Eddie's wife, for all that he admired, the flash of her face across a picket line – an attractive woman, but asleep." (p. 110)

Truman's helpless attraction to other white women than his wife is the dramatization of his own confusion when it comes to controlling his emotional life. As a critic puts it, "In Truman's failure to recognize the contradictions and inequities in his sexual ideology, he condemns himself to a spiritually tragic divisiveness"[56]. The couple's short-lived marriage or more specifically the reason why the man lost interest in the woman is used by the author as an opportunity to explore Truman's divided self:

> His feelings for Lynne had been undergoing subtle changes for some time. Yet it was not until the shooting of Tommy Odds in Mississippi that he noticed these changes. The shooting of Tommy Odds happened one evening just as he Truman, Tommy Odds and Trilling (a worker from Oklahoma since fled and never seen again) were coming out of the door of the Liberal Trinity Baptist Church. There had been the usual meeting with songs, prayers and strategy for the next day's picketing of downtown stores. They had assumed, also, that guards had been posted; not verifying was their mistake. As they stepped from the church and into the light from an overhanging bulb on the porch, a burst of machine-gun fire came from some bushes across the street. He and Trilling jumped off the sides of the steps. Tommy Odds, in the middle, was shot through the elbow. (p. 131)

The right mood is set when the event is briefly narrated that will serve as a catalyst for the big confrontation between Truman's private self and his public self. The irony of the situation as the author seems to articulate it here

---

56 Deborah E. McDowell : " The Self in Bloom : Alice Walker's *Meridian*." In CLA Journal, Vol xxiv #3, March 81, p. 269.

is that Mississippi which is regarded by Lynne herself as the best place to live the "Art" that she sees blacks as, the same Mississippi has now become the framework within which their love is to go through a trying experience. The events affecting their life as a couple originate from the confrontation between two races they didn't at first see themselves as the representatives of. Despite his previous decision, "after reading "le maître", that even "if he dated white girls it must be, essentially a matter of sex" there is ample evidence in the text that when he chooses to marry Lynne it is essentially because his private self has seen in her many qualities of love, personal dedication and political commitment that appealed to Truman. He "had felt hemmed in and pressed down by Lynne's intelligence." To be with her is therefore to express interest in an intellectual quest that implies a collective participation. But in retrospect, Lynne's contribution toward the shaping of Truman's character is not just intellectual:

> How marvelous it was at first to find that she read everything. That she thought, deeply. That she longed to put her body on the line for his freedom. How her idealism had warmed him, brought him into the world, made him eager to tuck her under his wing, under himself, sheltering her from her own illusions. Her awareness of wrong, her indignant political response to whatever caused him to suffer, was a definite part of her charm, and yet he preferred it as a part of her rarely glimpsed, commented upon in passing, as one might speak of the fact that Lenin wore a beard. (p. 140)

In this instance of focalization through Truman, the narrator tries to describe Lynne and ends up depicting her husband as well. One part of Lynne's personality revealed to Truman the urge for him to secure and save the other part by offering to protect her. The most important fact here is that she expresses her love for him by espousing a cause which has yet to be defined. In the context of the Civil Rights Movement the cause is the attainment of social justice and equality of opportunity for all. As a couple, unfortunately, they are part of a social network which imposes on events and attitudes meanings too often beyond their control. The mixed couple therefore becomes an easy ground where conflicting ethnic forces view the individual as a microcosm of a whole race. Truman cannot overlook the fact that Lynne's father disowned her on account of her choice. In addition, listening to the yellings of Lynne's mother who went to Truman's neighborhood to talk her daughter into returning home, one wonders whether the worst thing that can ever happen to a white couple is to "lose" their only daughter to a black man. Although they start out as two human beings who choose to be together because they can relate to each other, society makes sure that they perceive each other as the representatives of two different races.

On Truman's side of the race line, the energies mobilized to that effect are generated by his friends. When Truman visits with Tommy Odds at the hospital after the latter was fired at by a white gang, the conversation both of them have is crucial to the later development of Truman's character. His effort to include his wife ("Lynne says hurry up and get your ass out of here" (p. 132) in his social life is blatantly discouraged. "Don't mention that bitch to me" is the answer he receives from Tommy Odds. This symbolic way of erasing Lynne recalls to memory Guitar's purpose in joining the Seven Days. Truman, of course, cannot believe his ears. "Tommy Odds turned his head and looked at him, moving his lips carefully so there would be no mistake." And what he says this time around is "don't mention that white bitch." (p. 132) Shifting from "bitch" to "white bitch" is a way of indirectly subscribing to the attitude exhibited by Lynne's parents. The fight goes on. Truman is made to believe that his wife belongs with others. And if she does, it follows that he has deceived himself by making her his partner for life. The moment the problem is presented in terms of blacks versus whites, taking sides with Lynne is for Truman like excluding himself from the black community. His private self is at odds with what his public self – the mask society has had him put on – is supposed to be. Although he still feels committed to Lynne despite the decided effort of Tommy Odds acting on behalf of the black community as a group, his whole being is shaken. So even if he clearly suggests that "Lynne had nothing to do with this", the clash of the two sides of his split self-triggers off a most telling introspection. He has to choose between Lynne and blackness:

> While he was saying this, his tongue was slowed down by thoughts that began twisting like snakes through his brain. How could he say Lynne had nothing to do with the shooting of Tommy Odds, when there were so many levels at which she could be blamed? (p. 132)

It does not take Truman very long to figure out what Lynne may be guilty of:

> By being white Lynne was guilty of whiteness. He could not reduce the logic any further, in that direction. Then the question was, is it possible to be guilty of a color? Of course black people for years were 'guilty' of being black. Slavery was punishment for their crime'. But even if he abandoned this search for Lynne's guilt, because it ended, logically enough, in racism, he was forced to search through other levels for it. For bad or worse, and regardless of what this said about himself as a person, he could not – after his friend's words – keep from thinking Lynne was, in fact, guilty. The thing was to find out how. (p. 133)

Beyond the crucial question whether one can be guilty of a color, there seems to lurk a strategy being used by the author-narrator to drive home to her readers the nonsensical nature of the philosophical foundations of slavery as was experienced by black Americans. But evidently, the author does not want Truman holding Lynne guilty of whiteness. He, therefore, has to search through other levels for a sin to blame her for. Lynne, as the author sees her, is guilty until proven innocent. Truman is changing into a white-hater. In the process, however, he is soon confronted with the inconsistencies of his own line of arguments. The contradiction shows when his stand as a husband is scrutinized by the Civil Rights Movement activist engaged in building a society where one's race should not be regarded as a curse. In other words, by loading Lynne with a crime he cannot even define, he is indicating how far he has yet to go if he is to come to grips with the conflicting forces at work within him. Blackness erases his individuality as much as whiteness depersonalizes Lynne and sweeps away her Jewishness in the process. In fact even Truman sees no Jewish dimension to Lynne's existence at all. For him, she is just "an American white woman." Now she knows that whiteness as such does not generate the psychological protection that she needs and the sense of belonging that comes with it. No wonder people "make her conscious, heavily, of her Jewishness when, in fact they want to make her feel her whiteness." (p. 179) To try to strip Lynne of her Jewishness is to insist on the one striking, irreversible "difference" there is between the couple – skin color. Viewed from this angle, blackness is irreversible whereas Jewishness is not. As a matter of fact, one can even make the point that, for Truman, Jewishness is just a metaphor for suffering and persecution.[57] One may well imagine that as a Jew, she sees similarities between the Holocaust and the black experience. However, the interpretation now of those historical facts is not the same. It varies from one group to the other and within the same group, from one individual to the other. Lynne's marriage to Truman is therefore the affirmation of a personal stand. This is why Tommy Odds believes that Truman is just the means used by Lynne to teach her parents a lesson. A close analysis of the reasons why they fell in love with each other indicates that "her awareness of wrong" (p. 160) is just the manifestation of something in her that he never felt like figuring out. The truth of the matter is that by nature, she is not "cut out to be a member of the oppressors." (p. 181) She hates them because they make her feel guilty all the time. Her evaluation of her own growth as a person heavily depends on the dialectics of their common life as a couple and her statement that "Truman isn't much but he's "*instructional*" (p. 181) sheds some crucial light on the role he plays in exposing her to the condition of the oppressed. By committing himself to the Movement, he has openly expressed a concern, and the very statement thus made places him outside the community of ordinary people. His militancy is used by the author to help him mature into a new man. The image thus projected of him by Lynne is the culmination of the transformation the character has gone through ever since he joined the Movement.

However, from Meridian's standpoint, Truman has not always been a hero. He has not always been around to be supportive of her. As she was growing from the experiences and the facts of her own life, Truman was cold and distant. A juxtaposition of a number of episodes of the story shows that Truman's attraction to Meridian is, at first, now physical now ideological and always shallow. It becomes ideologically deeper only in response to peer pressure, that is when his friends start telling him that he is welcome among them as long as he does not come along with Lynne. Ironically enough, his ideological change appears to the character himself as an emotional growth. If he eventually seeks to part from his wife, it is not so much because he is now in love with Meridian as it is because he has developed a new attitude vis à vis "blackness". All things considered, Lynne also stays married to Truman for ideological reasons.

---

57 Members of both communities seem to agree with this view, which is why (like Julius Lester who holds that "there is no need for black people to wear yellow Stars of David on their sleeves; the Star of David is all over us,") Rabbi Alan Miller thinks that "The black man is, in truth, the American Jew." ; in Nat Hentoff, ed., *Black Anti-Semitism and Jewish Racism*, New York, Richard W. Barrow, 1969, pp. ix - x.

But this situation only aggravates Truman's psychological confusion. Viewed from that perspective, he now lives on the margins of mainstream American society. The author makes his position even more uncomfortable by using the two women's unbreakable friendship. In the name of this friendship, they freely share insights during their conversations which help once again to define Truman's character.

Despite Lynne's opinion that Truman saved her "from a fate worse than death," (p. 181) the fact of the matter is that he has not managed to save everybody that he came across. One case in point is Johnny the deer hunter and his wife (pp. 203 - 4) whom he fails to convince to register to vote:

> "What good is the vote if we don't own nothing?" asked the husband as Truman and Meridian were leaving. The wife, her eyes steadily caressing her husband's back, had fallen asleep, Johnny, Jr. cuddled next to her on the faded chenille bedspread. In winter the house must be freezing, thought Truman, looking at the cracks in the walls; and now, in spring, the house was full of flies.
>
> "Do you want free medicines for your wife? A hospital that'll take black people through the front door? A good school for Johnny, Jr. and a job no one will take away?"
>
> "You know I do," said the husband sullenly.
>
> "Well, voting probably won't get it for you, not in your lifetime," Truman said, not knowing whether Meridian intended to lie and claim it would.
>
> "What will it get me but a lot of trouble," grumbled the husband.
>
> "I don't know," said Meridian. "It may be useless. Or maybe it can be the beginning of the use of your voice. You have to get used to using your voice, you know. You start on simple things and move on..."
>
> "No," said the husband, "I don't have time for foolishness. My wife is dying. My boy don't have shoes. Go somewhere else and find somebody that ain't got to work all the time for pennies, like I do."

In reparation to a woman who had suffered such pain, Walker has explained: I liberated her from her own history... I wanted her to be happy" (Newsweek, 21 July 1982, p. 67). It is a clash between history and fiction, in part, that causes the problem with the novel.

On the way to making Celie happy, Walker portrayed her as a victim of many imaginable abuses and a few unimaginable ones.[63]

The first man Celie encounters is her stepfather who, despite her youth, fathers her two children. The image that Alice Walker makes Celie project of him in the first letter is repeated almost throughout the whole novel in the shape of different men. Fonso is the custodian of an authority and a power which he uses only for personal gains. He looks all the stronger as Celie is in position to stand up to him.

The author uses contrast over and again to depict the commanding role he in her life. Her silence not only protects her abuser against her mother's but by the same token, reinforces Fonso's position in the community. He spectable married man who is determined to preserve that appearance. es so by pretending and lying. The full story of his strategy of conquest is ally told years later, only after Celie has finished off verbalizing her pain a conversation with her husband's mistress, Shug. Before recording was raped by her stepfather whom she used to think was her own elie tells Shug the whole story:

he ast me, how was it with your children daddy?

e girls had a little separate room, I says, off to itself, connected he house by a little plank walk. Nobody ever come in there but na. But one time when mama not at home, he come. Told me anted me to trim his hair. He brings the scissors and comb and and a stool. While I trim his hair he look at me funny. He a ervous too, but I don't know why, till he grab hold of me and ne up tween his legs. (...)

through, I say, he make me finish trimming his hair. (...)

"Okay," said Meridian. Surprised, Truman followed calmly as she calmly walked away. (pp. 204 - 5)

This dramatization by Alice Walker of the necessity for blacks to make it a duty for them to vote fully makes sense in the context of the mood set by the author-narrator. But Truman's decision to be realistic and frank about what concrete changes voting can bring into the homes and lives of poor black people is manipulated by the author to show how the cycle of poverty is kept unbroken by the very people concerned. The result of the presentation, however, is a clear message for the black community that they can make their voices count. By failing to draw the conclusion personally, Johnny who sees no reason why poor people should vote is alienated by the author from American political life and is indirectly made to turn his back on some of the possibilities of having his lot improved. Johnny too is socially maladjusted.

Throughout the novel, the portrayal of the character Truman as a married man is presented through his propensity to involve himself in loyalty conflicts he cannot win. He maintains that despite the difficulties his marriage has been going through, he still loves Lynne; only that he does not desire her any more. This may very well explain why he fails to take the appropriate action when his wife was raped by his black friends. By allowing Truman to make such an irresponsible move, Alice Walker creates in the character a flaw that makes him a rapist of his own wife – morally speaking. This status brings him close to Grange Copeland, who did nothing to prevent Shipley from taking his wife. In Truman's case, though, the black man's failure to stand by his wife – if only symbolically – originates from a transfer of priority from "personal commitment" to what may be called "race allegiance." Once again, the author has managed, psychologically speaking, to make Truman a totally confused person. He does not know which way to turn anymore. As his control over the world around him dwindles, he appears more and more incapable of adapting himself to society and its rules. He gets caught by his wife having an affair with another white woman, gives up his former political commitment and asks Meridian to bear his black children. His last request seems to be of the greatest importance because it calls for an ideological reinterpretation of Truman's character as the rest of the story unfolds. In the Western tradition, it takes only one black parent to make a child black. In that respect, Camara, the daughter of Lynne and Truman, is as black as the children he could have with Meridian. Truman is therefore articulating here an ideological statement of a new kind. Having children with Meridian is seeing part of his soul reflected around him.

In other words, when considered from the triple perspective of Camara's death, her father's persistent attraction to white women, and his surprising desire to have Meridian bear his "black" children, the ideology of blackness that sustains the author's perception of the character Truman is evidently open to love, friendship, and sex across racial boundaries but frowns upon miscegenation and interracial marriages. Beyond this observation there also exists the fact that in the world of *The Third Life of Grange Copeland* and *Meridian*, Alice Walker's (married) men are always out to take advantage of women.

2.3 Humanizing The Black Man: An Analysis of *The Color Purple*

In her article titled "Saving the life that is your own: The importance of models In The artist's life,"[58] Alice Walker confesses that, just like Toni Morrison, she writes the kind of books she wants to read. One major feature common to novels like Toni Morrison's *Song of Solomon* and *Tar Baby* and Alice Walker's *Meridian* and The Color Purple is the female characters' successful attempts to go beyond the bitterness they have to deal with in the process of both trying to understand and explaining themselves to, the black men in their lives. This post-feminist perspective of theirs has the merit of sustaining a set of ideas that these two writers want reflected in the world of their fictions. This "ideology" Alice Walker locates in the double reality of the conception of creative ideas by individuals and the determination of these inventive generators to see their dreams materialize into concrete achievements. As she puts it: "… to write the books one wants to read is both to point the direction of vision and, at the same time to follow it."[59] A writer is a performer who acts out his/her own dreams. The vision "pointed" in *The Third Life of Grange Copeland* and elaborated on in *Meridian* is "followed" in *The Color Purple*.

The novel opens with the narrator's statement that "You better not never tell nobody but God. It'd kill your mammy." (p. 11) The sentence is deeply rooted in vernacular realities that the producer of it clearly wants to share with the reader. Syntaxically speaking Mem, at some stage of her personal growth in *The Third Life of Grange Copeland*, would not have recommended, syntaxically speaking, the type of language used in the letter. But the silent conversation between the letter writers and the author who, incidentally, regards herself

---

58 Alice Walker: In *Search of Our Mother's Garden*, pp. 3 - 14.
59 Alice Walker: In *Search of Our Mother's Garden*, p. 8.

as a medium (p. 253) underscores the necessity for the former to give shape and meaning to their lives by writing down their daily experiences in the ve[ry] language through which they were socialized into the values of the setti[ng]. The opening statement validates the language of the people concerned consequently makes it possible for them to feel comfortable using it in to tell their own stories. "The rootedness of the language in both the realities and the local socio-economic environment sustains the te the text and the unity of the stories."[60] And these stories can kill mammies because in substance they constitute an indictment of the tellers' lives. Only God can save them all. No wonder that Celi first letter begs God to "give me a sign letting me know what is me." (p. 11) As a set of texts sustained by a consistent sense of of cohesion, her diary may well be regarded as the first respor way to self-redeeming. Writing for her is, therefore, a way of her sufferings. It is an act of self-creation. By structuri daily life into meaningful pieces of what one may well call herself to engage in a reflection on the world around he people consistently treat her like a good-for-nothing men whose names she does not even know.

Alice Walker presents Celie's life as a steady su rejections and Celie's account of it reflects the na it miserable for her. They overpower her and kinds of transactions. As far as her own evalu the character Celie seems to have taken over wife, Mem, left off in *The Third Life of Gra* that a woman as black and therefore ugly Mister is internalized by Celie who sound worthlessness. Alice Walker "… has indic on her great-grandmother, who was master."[61] Elaborating on the above, T *Purple* as "a political shopping list of to repay,"[62] makes an important poi way black men are portrayed in th

---

60 M.A.K. Halliday, *Cohesion in Englis[h]*
61 Trudier Harris: " On The Colo[r]
Literature Forum, Vol. 18, Number
62 Ibidem, p. 160.

"Okay," said Meridian. Surprised, Truman followed calmly as she calmly walked away. (pp. 204 - 5)

This dramatization by Alice Walker of the necessity for blacks to make it a duty for them to vote fully makes sense in the context of the mood set by the author-narrator. But Truman's decision to be realistic and frank about what concrete changes voting can bring into the homes and lives of poor black people is manipulated by the author to show how the cycle of poverty is kept unbroken by the very people concerned. The result of the presentation, however, is a clear message for the black community that they can make their voices count. By failing to draw the conclusion personally, Johnny who sees no reason why poor people should vote is alienated by the author from American political life and is indirectly made to turn his back on some of the possibilities of having his lot improved. Johnny too is socially maladjusted.

Throughout the novel, the portrayal of the character Truman as a married man is presented through his propensity to involve himself in loyalty conflicts he cannot win. He maintains that despite the difficulties his marriage has been going through, he still loves Lynne; only that he does not desire her any more. This may very well explain why he fails to take the appropriate action when his wife was raped by his black friends. By allowing Truman to make such an irresponsible move, Alice Walker creates in the character a flaw that makes him a rapist of his own wife – morally speaking. This status brings him close to Grange Copeland, who did nothing to prevent Shipley from taking his wife. In Truman's case, though, the black man's failure to stand by his wife – if only symbolically – originates from a transfer of priority from "personal commitment" to what may be called "race allegiance." Once again, the author has managed, psychologically speaking, to make Truman a totally confused person. He does not know which way to turn anymore. As his control over the world around him dwindles, he appears more and more incapable of adapting himself to society and its rules. He gets caught by his wife having an affair with another white woman, gives up his former political commitment and asks Meridian to bear his black children. His last request seems to be of the greatest importance because it calls for an ideological reinterpretation of Truman's character as the rest of the story unfolds. In the Western tradition, it takes only one black parent to make a child black. In that respect, Camara, the daughter of Lynne and Truman, is as black as the children he could have with Meridian. Truman is therefore articulating here an ideological statement of a new kind. Having children with Meridian is seeing part of his soul reflected around him.

In other words, when considered from the triple perspective of Camara's death, her father's persistent attraction to white women, and his surprising desire to have Meridian bear his "black" children, the ideology of blackness that sustains the author's perception of the character Truman is evidently open to love, friendship, and sex across racial boundaries but frowns upon miscegenation and interracial marriages. Beyond this observation there also exists the fact that in the world of *The Third Life of Grange Copeland* and *Meridian*, Alice Walker's (married) men are always out to take advantage of women.

2.3 Humanizing The Black Man: An Analysis of *The Color Purple*

In her article titled "Saving the life that is your own: The importance of models In The artist's life,"[58] Alice Walker confesses that, just like Toni Morrison, she writes the kind of books she wants to read. One major feature common to novels like Toni Morrison's *Song of Solomon* and *Tar Baby* and Alice Walker's *Meridian* and The Color Purple is the female characters' successful attempts to go beyond the bitterness they have to deal with in the process of both trying to understand and explaining themselves to, the black men in their lives. This post-feminist perspective of theirs has the merit of sustaining a set of ideas that these two writers want reflected in the world of their fictions. This "ideology" Alice Walker locates in the double reality of the conception of creative ideas by individuals and the determination of these inventive generators to see their dreams materialize into concrete achievements. As she puts it: "... to write the books one wants to read is both to point the direction of vision and, at the same time to follow it."[59] A writer is a performer who acts out his/her own dreams. The vision "pointed" in *The Third Life of Grange Copeland* and elaborated on in *Meridian* is "followed" in *The Color Purple*.

The novel opens with the narrator's statement that "You better not never tell nobody but God. It'd kill your mammy." (p. 11) The sentence is deeply rooted in vernacular realities that the producer of it clearly wants to share with the reader. Syntaxically speaking Mem, at some stage of her personal growth in *The Third Life of Grange Copeland*, would not have recommended, syntaxically speaking, the type of language used in the letter. But the silent conversation between the letter writers and the author who, incidentally, regards herself

---

[58] Alice Walker: In *Search of Our Mother's Garden*, pp. 3 - 14.
[59] Alice Walker: In *Search of Our Mother's Garden*, p. 8.

as a medium (p. 253) underscores the necessity for the former to give shape and meaning to their lives by writing down their daily experiences in the very language through which they were socialized into the values of the setting. The opening statement validates the language of the people concerned and consequently makes it possible for them to feel comfortable using it in order to tell their own stories. "The rootedness of the language in both the ethnic realities and the local socio-economic environment sustains the texture of the text and the unity of the stories."[60] And these stories can kill the tellers' mammies because in substance they constitute an indictment of the men in the tellers' lives. Only God can save them all. No wonder that Celie in her very first letter begs God to "give me a sign letting me know what is happening to me." (p. 11) As a set of texts sustained by a consistent sense of different types of cohesion, her diary may well be regarded as the first responsible step on her way to self-redeeming. Writing for her is, therefore, a way of relieving herself of her sufferings. It is an act of self-creation. By structuring the story of her daily life into meaningful pieces of what one may well call literature, she forces herself to engage in a reflection on the world around her. This world in which people consistently treat her like a good-for-nothing is dominated by black men whose names she does not even know.

Alice Walker presents Celie's life as a steady succession of sufferings and rejections and Celie's account of it reflects the nature of the men who make it miserable for her. They overpower her and make her the object of all kinds of transactions. As far as her own evaluation of her self-esteem goes, the character Celie seems to have taken over where Brownfield Copeland's wife, Mem, left off in *The Third Life of Grange Copeland*. Brownfield's idea that a woman as black and therefore ugly as she is should be calling him Mister is internalized by Celie who sounds more than convinced of her own worthlessness. Alice Walker "... has indicated that the character Celie is based on her great-grandmother, who was raped at twelve by her slaveholding master."[61] Elaborating on the above, Trudier Harris, who refers to *The Color Purple* as "a political shopping list of all the I. O. Us Walker felt that it was time to repay,"[62] makes an important point in light of which I intend to look at the way black men are portrayed in this novel; she writes:

60 M.A.K. Halliday, *Cohesion in English* Chapter 1 (pp. 1-30)
61 Trudier Harris: " On The Color Purple, Stereotypes, and Silence," in Black American Literature Forum, Vol. 18, Number 4, Winter 84, p. 157.
62 Ibidem, p. 160.

> In reparation to a woman who had suffered such pain, Walker has explained: I liberated her from her own history... I wanted her to be happy" (Newsweek, 21 July 1982, p. 67). It is a clash between history and fiction, in part, that causes the problem with the novel.
>
> On the way to making Celie happy, Walker portrayed her as a victim of many imaginable abuses and a few unimaginable ones.[63]

The first man Celie encounters is her stepfather who, despite her youth, fathers her two children. The image that Alice Walker makes Celie project of him in the first letter is repeated almost throughout the whole novel in the shape of different men. Fonso is the custodian of an authority and a power which he uses only for personal gains. He looks all the stronger as Celie is in no position to stand up to him.

The author uses contrast over and again to depict the commanding role he plays in her life. Her silence not only protects her abuser against her mother's anger but by the same token, reinforces Fonso's position in the community. He is a respectable married man who is determined to preserve that appearance. He does so by pretending and lying. The full story of his strategy of conquest is eventually told years later, only after Celie has finished off verbalizing her pain during a conversation with her husband's mistress, Shug. Before recording how she was raped by her stepfather whom she used to think was her own father, Celie tells Shug the whole story:

> She ast me, how was it with your children daddy?
>
> The girls had a little separate room, I says, off to itself, connected to the house by a little plank walk. Nobody ever come in there but Mama. But one time when mama not at home, he come. Told me he wanted me to trim his hair. He brings the scissors and comb and brush and a stool. While I trim his hair he look at me funny. He a little nervous too, but I don't know why, till he grab hold of me and cram me up tween his legs. (...)
>
> After he through, I say, he make me finish trimming his hair. (...)

---

[63] Ibidem, p. 157.

> After while I say, Mama finally ast how come she find his hair in girls room if he don't ever go in there like he say. That when he told her I had a boyfriend. (pp. 108 - 109)

This incestuous relationship and how the man gets away with it constitute two different events which, once combined, give a clear indication of the type of morality Fonso stands for. Although the story is told from Celie's perspective, there is every indication that he knew that Celie thought he was her real father, which aggravates his situation as a rapist. If he is morally loose he is also good at falsifying any crucial facts that are likely to affect the image he wants people to see of him. The story of his "astuteness" is used as a source of knowledge to enhance Shug's familiarity with human nature. "Shug say, Wellsah, and I thought it was only whitefolks do freakish things like that." (p. 109) This piece of information later on helps shape her perception of her Albert, i. e. Celie's Mr _. The only experience Celie depends on to assess her husband's nature and personality is given shape in the suffering she endured at her stepfather's hand. A sketchy moral portrait of him is drawn in the third letter:

> Dear God,
>
> He act like he can't stand me no more. Say I'm evil an always up to no good. He took my other little baby, a boy this time. But I don't think he kilt it. I think he sold it to a man an his wife over Monticello. I got breast full of milk running down myself. He say Why don't you look decent? Put on something. But what I'm sposed to put on? I don't have nothing.
>
> I keep hoping he fine somebody to marry. I see him looking at my little sister. She scared. But I say I'll take care of you. With God help.

Celie's awareness of the man's power and the type of use he puts it to, indicates a clear sense of the limitations put on her. The dialectics of that power and Celie's powerlessness helps shape Fonso's profile as a socially maladjusted man throughout the text. The character Fonso, in the final analysis, is the powerful man that a tiny force like Celie eventually causes to disintegrate because he used to derive his strength from her ability to reassure him that she knows nothing. That she promises from her desperately isolated corner of the world to help her sister survive adds a heroic dimension to both the committed courage and the calculated abnegation she displays throughout the novel. "I ast him to take me instead of Nettie while our new mammy sick," she writes. This strategy aims to save her younger sister Nettie from falling prey to their stepfather's lust. It works at first. The picture of the stepfather, however, still has too many spots of indeterminacy to it. Most of the blanks are filled in when Celie records the first full length conversation he has with Albert (known to Celie simply as Mr_). Albert who was originally interested in Netty has to be content with Celie:

> Well, He say, real show, I can't let you have Nettie. She too young. Don't know nothing but what you tell her. Sides, I want her to git some more schooling. Make a schoolteacher out of her. But I can let you have Celie. She the oldest anyway. She ought to marry first. She ain't fresh tho, but I spect you know that. She spoiled. Twice. But you don't need a fresh woman no how. I got a fresh one in there myself and she sick all the time. She spit over the railings. The children get on her nerves, she not much of a cook and she big already.
>
> Mr_ he don't say nothing. I stop crying I'm so surprise.
>
> She ugly. He say. But she ain't no stranger to hard work. And she clean. And God done fixed her. You can do everything just like you want to and she ain't gonna make you feed it or clothe it.
>
> Mr_ still don't say nothing. I take out the picture of Shug Avery. I look into her eyes. Her eyes say yeah, it bees that way sometimes.
>
> Fact is, he say I got to git rid of her. She too old to be living here at home. And she a bad influence on my other girls. She'd come with her own linen. She can take that cow she raise down there back of the crib. But Nettie you flat out can't have. Not now. Not never.
>
> Mr_ finally speak. Clearing his throat. I ain't never really look at that one, he say.
>
> Well, next time you come you can look at her. She ugly. Don't even look like she kin to Nettie. But she'll make a better wife. She ain't

smart either, and I'll just be fair, you have to watch her or she'll give away everything you own. But she can work like a man.

Mr_ say how old she is?

He say, she near twenty. And another thing – she tell lies. (pp. 17 - 18)

While the use of reported speech lends more credibility to the images Alice Walker is promoting of the two men, Cellie's status as a negated human being is underlined by the final agreement reached by her bosses. This deal coldly struck between two men totally contemptuous of the reified Celie announces the transfer of power over her. She stands for a labor force that is valued by both parties. The form of enslavement this attitude promotes and encourages reflects the strictly materialistic mentalities of the men who display it. While the message seems clear that, once in a position of power, most oppressed people tend, in their turn, to hold weaker people down for whatever profit the situation can generate, it also implies that the value system sustaining the worldview of a community of people too often reflects almost exclusively the wishes and the dreams of the strong. The mule metaphor quite often used in black American literature (especially by black women writers) to describe the plight of black women is given substance as a result of the two men's determination to project a backward and undesirable image of Celie. From the two men's perspective the only positive point about her is that "she can work like a man;" (p. 18) and this point seems to be what makes her a better wife than Nettie. In fact, the definition of the term "wife" as a submissive mate readily willing to do only what she is ordered to, is the condition that places and keeps Celie at the bottom of the hiearachy of human beings as conceived by her stepfather. She is a nonentity he must get rid of. Mr_, the man who is to take over, is therefore set up to be cruel to Celie because, for one thing, he is made to perceive her as an unwanted person. Chances are Mr_ is going to be a replica of his future father-in-law. Not that it matters to Celie herself. As far as she can tell, "... mens look pretty much alike to me." (p. 23) The above statement evidently contrasts with the view of some people in the county that he is the nicest man around. Just like Fonso, Mr_ has a deceiving façade beyond which people usually fail to go. But when it comes to knowing Mr_, Celie is an insider.

Apart from Nettie, Celie has nobody in the world that she can love and feel loved by. Nettie is the only person who ever managed to make Celie feel "pretty cute." (p. 26) The role played by these two sisters in each other's lives is, therefore, exceptionally important. The heartless side to Mr_ takes a greater proportion when he decides to send away Nettie who came to stay with the couple. Not only is she very assertive but to top it off she has a vision. Her refusal to sleep with Mr_ is a big blow to a man who seems to take it for granted that he is entitled to anything he feels like. Once she is out of the way, Mr_ can freely do whatever he wants with Celie. In fact, his effort to erase both women clearly shows when, for several decades, he receives and holds Celie's letters from her sister living in Africa.

Originally it was indirectly said to Celie that she would be working like Mr_ when she first married him. Viewed from this angle, Mr_ fails to live up to her expectation. While Celie and Mr_'s son, Harpo, are in the field chopping and plowing all day, he sits back and watches them: "Why you don't work no more? He ast his daddy." Celie can never afford to ask such a question at this point of her life. In addition, she already knows the answer to it. Mr_, nevertheless, takes the trouble to reiterate it. "No reason for me to. His daddy say. You here, ain't you?" (p. 35) In her depiction of Harpo's interaction with his father, the author tells us a lot about men as she sees them. Her observation that Harpo is "strong in body but weak in will," (p. 35) implies that physical strength is all that "mens" have and they do use it to cover up their spiritual weakness.

The various signs Celie begs God for in her first letter are sent to her in the shapes of Shug, Nettie, and Harpo's wife. Both directly and indirectly, they prepare Celie to humanize her husband. But the most important achievement of hers seems to be her loss of interest in God and his replacement with Nettie, and it all happened when she and Shug eventually discovered the accumulated mail. The drastic change that occurs in the character coincides with the beginning of her acquisition of a keen sense of the urge to escalate from the passivity in which she has been grounded all her life in order to transcend what she considered her irremediable condition. She becomes articulate in her language and the result is a new Mr_.

Dear Nettie,

> I don't write to God no more, I write to you.
> What happen to God? Ast Shug.

> Who that? I say.
> She look at me serious.
>
> Big a devil as you is, I say, you not worried
> bout no God, surely.
>
> She say, Wait a minute. Hold on just a minute here. Just I don't harass it like some people us know don't mean I ain't got no religion.
>
> What God do for me? I ast
>
> She say, Celie! Like she shock. He gave you
> life, good health, and a good woman that love you
> to death.
>
> Yeah, I say, and he give me a lynched daddy, a crazy mama, a low down dog of a step pa and a sister I probably won't ever see again. Anyhow, I say, the God I been praying and writing to is a man. And act just like all the other mens I know. Trifling, forgitful and lowdown. (…) (p. 175)

Not only has she won the right to air her views but, in addition, she makes it clear that by her former silence she created a God out of every man she knew and put each of them on a pedestal. She is now prepared to break what she made. Actually, the author has been preparing her for this new mission ever since she (the author) decided to keep her sister Nettie away from Mr._. To be sure, Nettie does not leave Celie on her own accord. She leaves her sister because of situations and events engineered by Mr._. The irony, however, is that in his attempt to separate the two sisters Mr._ has simply contributed toward their reunion many years later.

As a matter of fact, Nettie leaves Celie only to run into "somebody" nice enough to give her a ride into town before pointing her "in the direction of the Reverend M_'s place." (p. 119) This Reverend – whom Harris ironically calls "(a) born again male feminist"[64] – is used by the author as a link between black American men and black African men. The author's decision to set the other half of the story in Africa underlines the pan-African nature of her enterprise.

64 Ibidem, p. 160.

As a matter of fact, the representation of Africa that most black Americans are familiar with is the one made available mostly by white Europeans and/or Americans. And, as Marion Berghahn notes, "only a very few Afro-Americans have actually succeeded in emancipating themselves completely from this 'white' image of Africa."[65] For an Afro-American novel to be set in black Africa, the author, therefore, must be making a statement by intentionally seeking to reappraise the old image of Africa.

Before the "expedition" reaches Olinkaland in West Africa, a series of letters were written by Nettie in which Alice Walker supplies all appropriate information about the background against which black men in the Black Continent will be portrayed. Nettie and the other missionaries have everything carefully planned before leaving America and she reminds her sister of it in her first letter from Africa:

> I never even thought about it as a real place, though Samuel and Corrine and even the children talked about it all the time.
>
> Miss Beasley used to say it was a place overrun with savages who didn't wear clothes. Even Corrine and Samuel thought like this at times. But they know a lot more about it than Miss Beasley or any of our other teachers, and besides, they spoke of all the good things they could do for the down-trodden people from whom they sprang. People who need Christ and good medical advice. (p. 122 - 123)

Clearly, Corrine and Sam, the missionaries, as the author has Nettie portray them here, are not on a fact-finding mission in Africa. Literacy and medical science have made them the custodians of a certain power and just like Fonso and Mr_ who like to decide on things and simply impose them on the women in their lives, the two black American missionaries "know" what Africans need. This patronizing attitude is a new version of the Eurocentrism displayed by white conquerors in colonial Africa. Oddly enough, in another letter, Nettie thinks "… Africans are very much like white people back home, in that they think they are the center of the universe…" (p. 155)) Nettie does not see any difference between her being a "missionary" in Africa and the

---

65 Marion Berghahn, *Images of Africa in Black American Literature*, Totowa, N. J., Rowman and Littlefield, 1977, p. 1.

traumatic experience that it means to the natives. To be sure, she notes that "Samuel ... reminded us that there is one big advantage we have. We are not white. We are not Europeans. We are black like the Africans themselves. And we and the Africans will be working for a common goal: the uplifting of black people everywhere." (p. 127) The panAfricanist overtone of the statement can be traced to the good intention of Sam and his followers. What leaves something to be desired, though, is the fact that there is no African input in the strategy to be adopted in view of the final objective. How to achieve this goal without turning the natives into outsiders in an African setting is not easy to articulate. Apart from this basic contradiction that she is part of, Nettie's discovery of black Africa is recorded in such a way that her letters invariably testify to her desire to share her newly gathered knowledge with her sister. "Oh, Celie, there are ... like ma was!!" (p. 126) But at times, Celie is just the symbolic pupil her sister tries to educate. Behind her (Celie's) frail figure one can see various audiences:

> Our work began to seem somewhat clearer in England because the English have been sending missionaries to Africa and India and China and God knows where all, or over a hundred years. And the things they have brought back! We spent a morning in one of their museums and it was packed with jewels, furniture, fur carpets, swords, clothing, even tombs from all the countries they have been. From Africa they have thousands of vases, jars, masks, bowls, baskets, statues – and they are all so beautiful it is hard to imagine that the people who made them don't still exist. And yet the English assure us they do not. Although Africans once had a better civilization than the European (though of course even do not say this: I get this from reading a man named J. A. Rogers) for several centuries they have fallen on hard times. "Hard times" is a phrase the English love to use, when speaking of Africa. And it is easy to forget that Africa's "hard times" were made harder by them. Millions and millions of Africans were captured and sold into slavery – you and me, Celie! (p. 129)

The rhetoric Nettie engages in here aims to remind blacks that they have a past they can derive pride from. In this other instance of focalization through Nettie, the author cites some to the sources she is basing her analysis on. The treatment of the evidence in the context of the letter contributes a lot toward the delineation of the background against which the African characters will be viewed later on by Nettie. In her evaluation of the socio-economic and political shape in which Africa currently is, she turns an accusing eye to the white people as well. Not many of them see a connection between the poor performance of present-day Africa on the stage of world affairs on the one hand and the slave trade, the colonial encounter, and their aftermath in the Black Continents on the other.

The series of questions that Nettie eventually writes down – why did they sell us? How could they have done it? And why do we still love them? – are elucidated and, in some cases, rephrased as she gets familiar with African realities. Her first real encounter is with the "blueblack" Senegalese.

> They are so black, Celie, they shine. Which is something else folks down home like to say about real black folks. But Celie, try to imagine a city full of these shining, blueblack people wearing brilliant blue robes with designs like fancy quilt patterns. Tall, thin, with long necks and straight backs. Can you picture it at all, Celie? Because I felt like I was seeing black for the first time. And Celie, there is something magical about it. Because the black is so black the eye is simply dazzled, and then there is the shining that seems to come really from moonlight, it is so luminous, but their skin glows even in the sun.
>
> But I did not really like the Senegalese I met in the market. They were concerned only with their sale of produce. (p. 131)

The language of fascination used by Nettie to describe blackness unquestionably contrasts with the repulsive implications it is associated with in most western white fiction. A comparison of Alice Walker's Africa with that of Joseph Conrad in *Heart of Darkness* or that of Joyce Cary in his "African novels" in general and *Mr Johnson* in particular gives a clear idea of the difference.

The narrator's fascination with Senegalese blacks, however, is spoiled by the latter's fascination with money. She was preceded in Senegal by capitalist ideology. Its political manifestation in Liberia translates into the love-hate relationship that the president, William Tubman, has with the "natives" who he views as a source of the problem more than anything else. By referring by name to the man who ruled Liberia for a quarter of a century, the author of *The Color Purple* adds a more realistic dimension to the background study of the world in which she intends to place her African characters. The president who is of Afro-American origin has his attitude toward his African countrymen sustained by a strategic amnesia that enables him to forget to appoint native African cabinet ministers. The fact that he has white ministers instead, clarifies his intentions as to whose interests he values most. The irony, though, is that although President Tubman and his Afro-American friends – none of whose "… wives could pass for natives" (p. 132) – seem to have acquired the feeling of belonging with the whites, all the cocoa fields across the country are owned by "people in a place called Holland." The Africans that Nettie meets in Olinkaland (p. 132) are therefore people alienated from their own lands; outsiders in their own country.

The first African man the author allows into the picture from the village the missionaries are supposed to settle in is a Christian Olinka, a combination of Africa and Europe. "His christian name is Joseph. He is short and fat, with hands that seem not to have any bone in them. When he shook my hand it felt like something soft and damp was falling and I almost caught it." (p. 138) This hopelessly soft portion of Africa with a Judeo-Christian nametag on it becomes the buffer between the newcomers and the muscular deep chocolate brown boatmen who, just like the blueblack Senegalese traders in Dakar, "paid very little attention to us …" (p. 139) Alice Walker's rhetoric of missed brotherhood once again points to a lack of spontaneity on the part of the natives especially the men. But once again what prevails very soon is black women's community of spirit: the first woman who eventually talks to them wants to know who the children's mother is. In her opinion, they both look like Nettie.

The narrator's depiction of Olinka men heavily depends on her perception of Olinka women. Having posited that "The Olinka do not believe girls should be educated," because "a girl is nothing to herself," (p. 144) the narrator moves on to describe women with a vision, i.e. mothers dragging their sons to the missionary school. Even young Olivia partakes of the women's vision when she proclaims that Olinka men are "like white people at home who don't want colored people to learn!" (p. 145) Since Alice Walker constantly compares whatever Nettie experiences in Olinkaland to what happens back in the United States, Olinka men eventually look like their American brothers in that they don't know that "the world is changing," that "it is no longer a world just for boys and men." (p. 148) How short-sighted and socially maladjusted Olinka men are is dramatized in a conversation between Nettie and Tashi's father, who does not want Tashi educated in the western ways.

> Our Women are respected here, said the father. We would never let them tramp the world as American women do. There is always someone to look after the Olinka woman. A father. An uncle. A brother or nephew. Do not be offended, sister Nettie, but our people pity women such as you who are cast out, we know not from where, in a world unknown to you, where you must struggle all alone, for yourself.
>
> So I am an object of pity and contempt, I thought, to men and women alike.
>
> Furthermore, said Tashi's father, we are not simpletons. We understand that there are places in the world where women live differently from the way our women do, but we do not approve of this different way for our children.
>
> But life is changing, even in Olinka, I said.
> We are here.
> He spat on the ground.
> What are you? Three grownups and two children. In the rainy season some of you will probably die. You people do not last long in our climate. If you do not die, you will be weakened by illness. Oh, yes. We have seen it all before. You Christians come here, try hard to change us, get sick and go back to England, or wherever you come from. Only the trader on the coast remains, and even he is not the same white man, year in and year out. We know because we send him women. (p. 149)

The death of Tashi's father, in view of his stand on women's place and role in Olinka ssociety, appears as a device used by the author to remove a major obstacle from Tashi's way to self-fulfillment as defined by the narrator. In her prescription, Nettie rules out, among other practices, polygamy because, for one thing it takes romance out of the women's lives and for another it turn Olinka men into childish adults. (p. 153) The author's decision to change this scheme of things brings in Samuel. She thinks it his "duty as a Christian minister to preach the bible's directive of one husband and one wife." (p. 153) This naïve way of trying to use the bible for feminist purposes within the community overlooks the fact that the bible itself is but a collection of statements that can be used by different people to different ends. All it takes is to generate the right kind of rhetoric that validates one's claims. Samuel's skepticism about the mission being imposed on him by Nettie reflects his own inner doubts. He "is confused because to him, since the women are friends and will do anything for one another – not always, but more often than anyone from America would expect – and since they giggle and gossip and nurse each other's children, then they must be happy with things as they are." (p. 153) Clearly, Alice Walker is having Samuel's conception of happiness among Olinka women read like insensitiveness to the plight of African women as the narrator sees it. Samuel's point, however, is all the more understandable as, back in America, Mr_ has been in a monogamous marriage for years without ever having Celie experience anything close to the Olinka type of happiness. Romance, Samuel seems to imply, is not love. It is just a way of expressing it that happens to be very popular in the Western world. His conception also reiterates his position as an outsider who does not want to be a vector of change in every aspect of Olinka life. Nevertheless, the author sends him on a civilizing mission among Olinka men. Elaborating on the author's idea that men in Olinkaland are often childish Netty writes:

> And a grown child is a dangerous thing, especially since among the Olinka, the husband has life and death power over the wife. If he accuses one of his wives of witchcraft or infidelity, she can be killed.
>
> Thank God (and sometimes Samuel's intervention) this has not happened since we have been here. (p. 153)

Olinka men as Alice Walker sees them are backward, selfish phallocrats committed, just like their black American brothers, to keeping down nice, innocent Olinka women – a replica of the author's black American women. In *The Color Purple* Samuel goes to Africa, among other things, to "humanize" his brothers in the same way black American women have the responsibility of humanizing black American men. In so doing, he teaches a philosophy of action that brings into question the role played by men in traditional Olinkaland.

But Samuel is not the only one who is out to humanize in *The Color Purple*. Shug and Mr_'s wife evidently join forces to humanize Mr_ and so do Celie and Harpo's wife, Harpo. The image of a helpless Harpo crying because his wife Sofia has deserted him on account of the ill treatment he has been giving her (p. 65) is an indication of the necessity for him to be educated as to how a husband should treat his wife. Celie, at first, turned to Shug for emotional comfort because of Mr_'s inability to connect with her - both sentimentally and psychologically. In either case, the author has the men eventually face the pettiness of their own lives by confronting them with the belated psychological maturity of the women in their existence.

If Fonso is not Celie's father, Adam is still their son. The new situation simply changes Fonso's status from "incestuous father" to "polygamous husband". The character Adam is portrayed by Alice Walker as the one black American man who eventually does what the Liberian men of American descent will not do: marry a native African woman. In so doing he plays a determining role in the engineering of Tashi's voluntary exile in America. The author uses him to complete the last leg of a "triangular trade" era. Only this time around, the "captive" is made to perceive the whole experience as a migration of the heart. Most of Alice Walker's black men as are portrayed in *The Color Purple* operate under limitation of information and vision, especially when dealing with women. In the light of the above, their lives as socially maladjusted individuals fully make sense. At the same time their existence seems written against the background of an unclear message of optimism that once they know any better, they will move onto higher planes. In Alice Walker's first three novels, the author's project has constantly been to have her black women overcome (male) adversity. In the world of her fiction, men exhibit a limited vision which almost always prevents them from seeing beyond their own petty, present interests. Unlike Toni Morrison whose fiction allows room for individual expression, Alice Walker in her description of black males has a Manichean perspective which makes most of her characters carry invariably the burden of gender.

3

BLACK MEN IN THE FICTION OF TONI CADE BAMBARA

BLACK MEN IN THE FICTION OF TONI CADE BAMBARA

Toni Cade Bambara's few short stories and one novel discussed here read like a very sophisticated attempt to level out most of the imbalances spotted by both Toni Morrison and Alice Walker in the black communities of their various novels. Boyboy, Macon Dead and Son are just three faces of the psychologically crippled black man depicted by Toni Morrison in her fiction discussed in this study. This black man has evolved into a socially maladjusted monster to be educated by dedicated women like Mem, Meridian, Lynne and Celie in Alice Walker's first three novels. The way Alice Walker routinely shapes her women clearly makes inevitable her black male characters' dependence – on these women – for any positive attitude towards life. This tendency to idealize black women takes different forms in the fiction of most black women novelists, which is why Ishmael Reed, a black male novelist and literary critic, ironically observes that black women novelists fill their books with "ghetto women who can *do no wrong*."[66]

Bambara's black men are ordinary people caught up in a network of political choices and moral ideals informed by the author's ideological declaration of intent that makes the black community's survival, as a united whole, a duty of the highest importance. As a writer of fiction, Toni Cade Bambara engages in promoting a strategy that purports to establish the necessity for the artist to be a fighter. The role she assigns the creative writer is unconditionally political,

---

[66] John Domini, "Roots and racism: an interview with Ishmael Reed", *Boston Phoenix*, 5th April 1977, p. 20.

especially when scrutinized in the light of her own commitment:

> Through writing I attempt to celebrate the tradition of resistance, attempt to tap Black potential, and try to join the chorus of voices that argues that exploitation and misery are neither inevitable nor necessary. Writing is one of the ways I practice the commitment to explore bodies of knowledge for the usable wisdoms they yield.[67]

Her desire to channel the energies of blacks along new avenues likely to lead to the dismantling of the prevailing political order constitutes what she refers to as 'the message'. As a self-proclaimed "brazenly 'message' writer"[68] she points to the "healing possibilities" available to blacks by bringing together their spiritual strength and their political awareness. She operates from the premise that even in literature, "(t)he 'experts' are still men, black or white. And the images of the woman are still derived from their needs, their fantasies, their second-hand knowledge…"[69] To try to set the record straight is to engage in reconstructing black identity. Redefining black identity means, to Toni Cade Bambara, projecting a feminist perception of women in their interaction with both men and fellow women and she is fully aware of the importance of the task to be performed : "The job of purging is staggering. It perhaps takes less heart to pick up the gun than to face the task of creating a new identity, a self, perhaps an androgynous self, via commitment to the struggle."[70]

Although the gender politics of Morrison, Walker, and Bambara rest, in essence, on the same ideological foundation, each of these writers is original in her depiction of the black community and the role played by men in it. Like Toni Morrison's, Toni Cade Bambara's fiction posits that the black man's aspirations in the context of American society cannot materialize until he decides to acknowledge the black woman's contribution towards their common future. Unlike Morrison, however, Bambara does not, as a rule, set up her female characters to trap their men in an attempt to establish female visibility. Like Alice Walker, Toni Cade Bambara writes against a psychology of blackness that stresses the common destiny underneath the various individual choices made by each member of the black community; unlike

---

67 Toni Cade Bambara: "What I think I'm Doing Anyhow", in Janet Sternburg, ed., *The Writer on Her Work*, New York, W. W. Norton & Co., 1980, (p. 154).
68 Ibidem. (p. 161).
69 In *The Black Woman*, Toni Cade Bambara, ed., (p. 9).
70 Ibid. (p. 103).

Walker, Bambara does not allow the individual choices to work irremediably against the cohesion of the community.

In "The Hammer Man",[71] the narrator depicts Manny the "hammer man" as one who does not waste time verbalizing his feelings. No wonder "... after I called him what I called him and said a few choice things about his mother..." he does not say anything. Only "... his face did go through some piercing changes." (p. 35) Manny appears as a focused individual who quickly decides what to do when confronted with a specific situation. In the case of the narrator's name calling, Manny's decision is to strike back – not by insulting back – and the fact that the message of his project is relayed by the narrator's father is indicative of Manny's audacity. Although the author does not involve directly the narrator's father in the fight that the narrator started without meaning to, she manages to convey a sense of what she assumes the men's duty is:

> My father got in on it too, cause he happened to ask Manny one night why he was sitting on the stoop like that every night. Manny told him right off that he was going to kill me first chance he got. Quite naturally this made my father a little warm, me being his only daughter and planning to become a doctor and take care of him in his old age. So he had a few words with Manny first, and then he got hold of the older brother, who was more his size. Bernard didn't see how any of it was his business or my father's business, so my father got mad and jammed Bernard's head into the mailbox. Then my father started getting messages from Bernard's uncle about where to meet him for a showdown and all. My father didn't say a word to my mother all this time ... (p. 37).

At first, the world depicted here by the author looks totally like a man's world. Fathers, uncles, nephews, sons and brothers are the custodians of an unvoiced order that is supposed to prevail at all cost. They are in charge of all the action and they dutifully perform it to their own satisfaction. As a result, the women appear as mere on-lookers. The female narrator, however, presents herself as one who is determined to break into this male-dominated world. As a self-appointed potential protector of her father in his old age, she indirectly points to an assumed resignation of her brothers. This assumed resignation

---

71 In *Gorilla, My Love* (pp. 33 - 34).

later on turns into a symbolic reality acted out by Manny on a basketball court. It is interesting to note that the snow-ball effect of the fight initiated by the narrator brings together only men eager to show each other what they are up to. Bernard, who prefers to let individuals take care of their own problems, eventually sounds out of place in the picture because he fails to abide by the rule that whatever concerns the individual must concern the male members of the community: to fight one's child's fight is to acknowledge one's role in the community.

The same perspective prevails when the narrator and Manny are harassed by the police on a basketball court late one night. When one of the two white policemen refers to Manny as "black boy", the black woman's reaction sets the tone for the rest of the story: "now, when somebody says that word like that, I gets warm. And crazy or no crazy, Manny was my brother at that moment and the cop was the enemy." (p. 40) The narrator's determination to establish to the fullest the manhood being denied the Hammer Man comes as no surprise. Her willingness to be part of the men's world is given a chance to materialize. Manny's readiness to stand on his own feet as a "man" inside the black community contrasts with his resignation when faced with the white policemen. The series of events that lead to the narrator's above mentioned ideological pronouncements establish the black woman as the one who keeps the spirit of the struggle alive as opposed to the black man who appears to be very efficient only when it comes to taking punctual actions. Manny, the over-focused basketball player just hangs around and lets his "sister" fight his fight in his stead. She acts up to his unexpressed expectation by systematically taking all the questions put by the policemen to both of them. The narrator plays her role so well she eventually transforms talking into the only appropriate action worth undertaking under the prevailing circumstances. The irony of the situation lies in the fact that Manny's silence tends to "confirm" the policemen's conviction that the couple got sexually involved in the park, whereas the true story as told by the narrator sounds like an effort on her part to camouflage what the policemen take to be the self-evident truth. The reader's sense of what the character Manny is actually about is informed by the narrator's determination to not allow the "system" to jeopardize his future: "'You better give him back his ball,' I said." The role of passive on-lookers assigned to black women by black men as suggested earlier on by the author, is squarely ignored by a black woman who, ironically enough, feels more comfortable challenging the two white men more than the black man does. "Manny don't take no mess from no cops. He ain't bothering nobody. He's gonna be Mister Basketball when he grows up. Just trying to get a little practice in before the softball season starts." (p. 40)

The rhetoric of black brotherhood permeating the whole story is eventually represented in the shape of an unconditional gift from the black woman to the black man in front of outside adversity. Manny's girlfriend knows the inside story of his past and present as much as that of his dream for the future. In brief, he can "tell" his future image, which makes her, if temporarily, his "creator." Although the two law enforcement agents ignore the woman's statement, Manny's silence indirectly makes it the only alternative "image" they have of him that is not grounded in their own prejudice. Prior to the expression by the narrator of this emotional bond, Manny was aggressive, articulate in his own way, and more action-oriented than anything else. And one way he tries to convey a sense of his being is by planning on teaching a black woman a lesson. Inside the black community, he deserves the name "Hammer Man", especially when one looks at him from the perspective of the people he can easily beat up. Outside the community, though, he is psychologically handicapped by forces beyond his control. His initiation into manhood – by the standard of American society as a whole – includes among other phases, a close contact with the world outside the black community. The path is less difficult to travel if he makes the black woman his journey companion. Even though he gets arrested by the police, the reader understands that Manny is not alone. The same sense of belonging that Manny is supposed to experience is much more emphatically articulated in "A Tender Man", another story by Toni Cade Bambara.

"A Tender Man"[72] is the story of Cliff – a black man once married to a white woman named Donna. Rhea, their daughter, was born while he was fighting in Cuba as an American soldier. Cliff, now a divorced sociology instructor, is attracted to Aisha, a black woman who is more than determined to take Rhea from her white mother and raise her as a black child.

Thematically the story partly reminds one of Alice Walker's *Meridian*. Just like Truman, the character Cliff eventually disapproves of his own choice of partner. However, unlike Alice Walker who astutely uses Camara's death as a device to free Truman from his married past, Toni Cade Bambara keeps Rhea alive and focuses on the necessity for the father to prove responsible enough to help raise the mulatto girl.

---

72 In *The Sea Birds Are Still Alive*, pp. 125 - 151).

The psychological portrait of Cliff as a would-be father shows that the character is not sure what his relationship with his daughter will be like. The narrator even implies that Cliff, on the ship carrying him to a war he does not think he can survive, has taken all appropriate dispositions "He had pronounced the marriage null and void in the spring of '61. On the troop ship speeding to who knew where, or at least none of the dudes in that battalion knew yet, but to die most probably." (p. 138) For the character as he now stands, if he still has a future at all, there is no place in it for a child. Cliff is simply avoiding what Michael G. Cooke calls 'intimacy', which takes in Afro-American literature "the form of reaching, or being invited, out of the self and into an unguarded and uncircumscribed engagement with the world."[73] From her father's perspective, therefore, Rhea at one point is an unwanted child, which is why Cliff "... read the letter over and over and was convinced Donna was lying about being pregnant and so far advanced." (p. 138) Not only is he limited in his movements as a result of his presence on a ship but he is also psychologically held hostage by a past he cannot run away from. Even his future looks mortgaged:

> Cliff had collapsed on his bunker, back pack and all, the letter crumpling under his ear. A child was being born soon, the letter said. He was going to be a father. And if he died, what would happen to his child? His marriage had been in shreds before he'd left, a mere patchwork job on the last leave, and she'd been talking of going home. His child. Her parents. That world. Those people. (pp. 139 - 40)

The story of Rhea's unplanned beginnings is told by the narrator as a flashback destined to shed some more light on Cliff's current inner conflict. She is now standing on the borderline between a territory she is familiar with, and "that world." She is the unavoidable link between him and himself and "those people". Bambara makes Cliff perceive his own child as a combination of two conflicting realities.

The point is made in many subtle ways that the character Cliff is very anxious to be accepted by Aisha the black woman he now wants to get involved with. Fear of rejection, consequently, makes him feel judged or

---

[73] Michael G. Cooke, *Afro-American Literature in the Twentieth Century*, New Haven, Yale university Press, 1984, p. 9.

evaluated whenever interracial relationships are discussed. "He had enough of the white girl-brother thing. Had been sick of it all, of hearing, reading about it, of arguing, of defending himself, even back then on the tail end of the bohemian era, much less in the Black and Proud times since." (p. 140) Throughout the crucial conversation he has with Aisha in a restaurant Cliff behaves up to the narrator's idea of him as it is expressed in the foregoing statement. He wants to live in the present as a self-detached from the Cliff of the past, which is one reason he keeps on specifying that Donna is his ex-wife. The unreliable narrator soon makes the black woman locate what looks like a mask on the black man's face:

> "Cliff?" She seemed to call to him, the him behind his poker face. He leaned forward. Whatever she had to say, it'd be over with soon and they could get on with the Friday evening he had in mind.
>
> "I asked Donna on Tuesday to give up the child. To give your daughter to me. I'm prepared to raise _"
>
> Cliff stared, not sure he heard that right. (p. 140 - 41)

Cliff is interested in the here and now whereas Aisha is standing tall, scrutinizing the future and trying, in the process, to help him stand up. The irony here is that the attitude Aisha takes indicates that Cliff, in her opinion, is not mature enough to stand on his own feet. The theme of power-play as introduced by Bambara in the conversation, sheds light, once again, on the back woman's confidence that she can succeed where the black man fails. In fact she defines, in her own terms, "irresponsibility" in the black man's behavior. In the narrator's presentation Aisha eventually decides to take care of Rhea because the latter's white mother has been too much looking up to her for advice on "black" matters. Donna's determination to raise her daughter as a black child is clearly indicative of the black father's failure to live up to many people's expectations. Viewed from this perspective, Aisha's question to her white colleague Donna: "Where is the nigger daddy who should be taking the weight?" (p. 142) is both an homage to Rhea's mother and an indictment of Cliff, especially when the latter is seen against the background of his present obsession as it is articulated by the narrator. Cliff changes his mind and decides that "she was a type ... he didn't like ..." although he still thinks that he "... might take her home to make love to her – no, to fuck her." The narrator's explanation for all this is that "she kept him off balance." (p. 142) The fact of the matter is that Bambara is depicting a world where the black man resents the questions put to him by the black woman because he cannot answer them without pointing to his own limitations and, consequently, running the risk of jeopardizing his relationship with her. As the author seems to insinuate, Cliff's treatment of his white ex-wife is a foretaste of whatever Aisha might have to cope with one day as his partner. At least, this is the way Bambara has Cliff assess the woman's inquisitive behavior. As a result, the atmosphere keeps on changing – just like the black man's feelings.

Cliff's conquest strategy is destroyed by a clever Aisha who, in so doing, clearly indicates that her priority of the moment is black parents' responsibility to their children. Toni Cade Bambara, here, is simultaneously depicting two different types of "intimacy": one is both moral and psychological, the other is physical and shallow. Aisha's commitment is the political expression of a psychological healing process engineered by her in view of bringing home to Cliff an ultimate quest, a crucial "message" that the black man has no right to ignore: "… no matter when or where or how we met, the father question would've come up …" (p. 142) The narrator makes Aisha's control of the situation so total she takes the lead throughout the whole story. She refers to him indiscriminately as "sugar", "mister", or "brother" depending on her mood. She can afford to be ironical, formal, or shockingly straightforward if she so wishes. As a result, the discourse she has been producing goes far beyond the mere verbal representation of Cliff's character and sheds different lights on the space he has created between himself and the rest of the black community. As she sees it, Cliff's initiation into manhood implies a journey back home. From his perspective, though, Aisha's evaluation of him is totally wrong. "He wasn't sure for what, but he felt he was being unjustly blamed for something." (pp. 143 - 4) The narrator has constantly placed Aisha and Cliff on two different planes with Aisha always playing the finer role. The man's unawareness of these two levels of discourse results in his poor timing as far as his move on Aisha goes. Their priorities of the moment are basically different and since most of the talking has been done by the woman, the man takes it for granted that he knows the type of person his interlocutor is. With this in mind, the narrator has him mentally jump to a most important conclusion about her:

> She wasn't going to sleep with him, that was clear. He knew from past experiences that the moment had passed, that moment when

women resolved the tension by deciding yes they would, then relaxed one way, or no they wouldn't, and eased into another rhythm. (p. 144)

But his past knowledge of women is proven wrong when applied to Aisha. In light of the foregoing, Keith E. Byerman's observation is right: Toni Cade Bambara "… tends to leave her characters at the edge of some new experience rather than with a sense of the completion of action…"[74]

Toni Cade Bambara has often insisted that she values whatever brings blacks together over what divides them. In "A Tender man" poor timing has made Cliff perceive the black woman as a bossy, exceedingly aggressive person who wants to teach the black man how to behave properly. Fortunately, he is rescued from his misperception by Aisha as the story draws to an end. The truth of the matter is that both characters are attracted to each other. The only difference is the woman's strong desire to have their relationship sustained by a deep sense of responsibility and self-respect. As can be seen in this story, the black woman has a crucial role to play in the black man's initiation into manhood. Aisha is more than a nurse; she is a healer.

The same role is played in a more sophisticated way by Velta, Ruby and other very observant black women in Toni Cade Bambara's first novel.[75] The sophisticated style of the author of *The Salt Eaters* and the complex structure of the novel are combined to shed a variety of lights on the crucial contributions of black women toward a redefinition of black manhood. The survival of the black community as a cultural entity capable of generating a political force, is the obsession of most of the female characters. Ruby's assessment of the lack of cohesion in the community comes, therefore, as no surprise: "I dunno. Malcom gone, King gone, Fanni Lou gone, Angela quiet, the movement splintered, enclaves unconnected. Everybody off into the Maharaji. This and the Right Reverend That. If it isn't some far-off religious nuttery, it is some otherworldly stuff…'" (p. 193) The atomization and the chaos described by Toni Cade Bambara – here from the point of view of a committed black woman who scrutinizes the black community as a whole – are what the novel seeks to replicate. Paradoxically enough, the lack of cohesion does not result in confusion. Not on the women's side of the gender gap, anyway.

---

[74] Fingering the Jagged Grain, (p. 105).
[75] The Salt Eaters. (New York: Vintage Books), 1981. All subsequent quotations are taken from this edition.

> "... let's face it" (Ruby) said from under the table, "Women for Action is taking on entirely too much: drugs, prisons, alcohol, the schools, rape, battered women, abused children. And now Velma's talked the group into tackling the nuclear power issue. And the Brotherhood ain't doing shit about organizing." (p. 198)

The long list of what women have been doing and the contrasting passivity of black men are portrayed as the two sides of the same coin. In the process of describing this dichotomy, Toni Cade Bambara clearly indicates that, at times, knowledge in view of internal growth may well flow from black women towards black men. No wonder the reader is informed that black men's inaction affects black women's very existence. As Ruby puts it: " ' (b)ecause men jive around with each other instead of dealing for real and later for all the beating-on-the-chest raw gorilla shit, all the unresolved stuff slops over into man/woman relationships.'" (p. 199)

Against this background of female skepticism as to men's willingness to address the major issues facing (black) American society James Lee Henry, called Obie, and a few other black males are portrayed by Toni Cade Bambara. Velma expects her husband James to commit himself to the cause of the community on the one hand and on the other hand to make himself available to her whenever she needs him. As far as his commitment to her goes, she is not fully satisfied and although the dramatization of this state of affair is set in a restaurant, it directly focuses on the couple's private life. Against the background of a heart-felt nostalgia the author opens a window onto a world where the sweet responses provoked in James back in the past by Velma's very presence are now mere memories contrasting with the reality of her present life. Thus, although she has on "(t)he kind of blouse that years ago she would have worn to put James Lee Henry, called Obie now, under her spell," she must live with the internal certainty that " (h)e no longer thought she was a prize to win." (p. 20) During the confrontation between husband and wife the images projected of the two characters and the various symbols sustaining them tell the story of James's internal change. The author suggests that Velma, who once attempted suicide, now tries to "withdraw the self to a safe place where husband, lover, teacher, workers, no one could follow, probe. Withdraw herself and prop up a broderguard to negotiate with would-be intruders." (p. 5) Obie is aware that his wife almost killed herself because of the pressure resulting from the redeeming role she wanted to play in all these people's lives.

And yet, the author's intention seems to turn him into an intruder. A hard one to negotiate with:

> James Lee had begun moving the dishes aside, disrupting her meal. Her salad bowl no longer under her right wrist where she could get at it between chunks of steak and mouthfuls of potatoes but shoved up against the wall next to the napkin rack. Her sweet potato pie totally out of reach. And now he moved her teacup toward the hot sauce bottle. He was interrupting her story, breaking right in just as she was about to get to the good part, to tell her to put her fork down and listen. (p. 21)

The active search, on Jame's part, for a friction between himself and Velma manifests itself in the double attempt to symbolically starve her on the one hand and to prevent her from talking, on the other hand. But the dislocation by him of the precarious order prevailing in her inner universe is not an end in itself. It is, instead, a way of testing the foundation upon which that universe rests. Not only does the author allow James in this private universe of Velma's, but in addition, he applies more pressure on her as if to push her against the wall: "He was making an appeal, a reconciliation of some sort, conditions, limits, an agenda, help. Something about emotional caring or daring or sharing..." (pp. 21 - 22) The psychological profile of the character is more concretely depicted as he engages in a conversation with his wife:

> "We're different people, James. Obie. Somebody shit all over you, you forgive and forget. You start talking about how we're all damaged and colonialism and the underdeveloped blah blah. That's why everybody walks all over you."
>
> You're the only one to ever try to walk over me, Vee."
>
> "That's why I just can't stay with you. I don't respect – "
>
> "That's not why, Vee.
>
> "What?"

"Scared. Anytime you're not in absolute control, you panic."
"Scared?" She chewed with her mouth open, certain the sight would make him shut up or at least turn away. "Shit. Scared of you? Sheeeeet. Obie."

"Intimacy. Love. Taking a chance when the issue of control just isn't –" (p. 23)

By allowing Obie to know how Velma feels without her having to tell him, the author equips the character with the means he needs to improve his performance as a husband. Had an argument of this nature taken place between Pauline and Cholly Breedlove in Toni Morrison's *The Bluest Eye*, it would have changed the couple's life; for better that is. The fact of the matter is that Morrison and Bambara, at some point, have confronted both husbands with situations which are similar in the sense that each situation results from a power struggle between both spouses. But while Morrison allows the disintegration of a man reduced to a toy by a manipulating wife, Bambara makes Obie aware of his wife's destructive project, which enables him to short-circuit her. This foreknowledge of what Velma is about does not, however, turn Obie into an oppressive, inconsiderate husband willing to strike back. Misusing this information would have brought him very close to Alice Walker's Brownfield Copeland in *The Third Life of Grange Copeland* or Mr_ in *The Color Purple*. Instead, sharing this information with his wife brings him closer to her.

Despite the strict order around which it is structured, Velma's inner self is not the only world that needs protection from intruders. Like Obie, Dr Meadows is represented by Bambara as an intruder. Only in his case the structure he risks disrupting does not refer to one individual. Instead, Dr Meadows is portrayed as a threat to the inner organization that sustains aspects of black identity and black people's self-apprehension. He is a lonely man who stands in a category almost by himself. When the author describes him on his way to the Infirmary one evening, the character "found himself daydreaming on a family he'd never had." He seems forced by circumstances to make up "things to keep himself company." (p. 176) This may well explain why he has black community. Dr Meadows' commitment is all the more meaningful as he is light enough in complexion to pass as a White. As a matter of fact, his nose seems to be the one remaining "black" feature that he still has. The narrator ironically laments the fact that years of dutiful nose pinching carefully monitored by Dr Meadows' mother failed to make him a Caucasian. Dr Meadows conscious rejection of his mother's choice is not undertaken without the awareness that, racially, whatever he feels he is may not be obvious to everybody. His situation becomes understandably more precarious when he goes to places where he is not known:

> Meadows would have preferred a walk in the woods. Stumbling about aimlessly amidst trees and squirrels on the hunt for the essential selves of the patient and the healer would not have been nearly so alarming as fumbling along the pavement, crossing streets for no reason, attracting attention to his foreignness, attracting danger. To walk in the woods, one needed a gun, just a prop to guise the meandering. In these unknown streets, who knew what he needed?

The various people he is made to interact with in these unknown streets see almost everything in black and white. As a result, they turn his life into a perpetual dilemma. The author repeatedly uses flashbacks and flashforwards to account for the character's current state of mind. A multitude of mental images and old memories mingle in his mind in an attempt to help bridge the gaps between Meadow's past, his present, and his future. While he remains confronted with the ordeal of living with an appearance reflecting another reality than the one he feels deep inside him, Meadows scrutinizes Claybourne. Unlike Meadows, the town "hadn't settle on its identity yet… Its history puts it neither on this or that side of the Mason Dixon." (p. 181) Depending, therefore, on where one is in Claybourne, one could be on one side or the other of the Mason Dixon line. The section of the town where most of the action is set is "Where the poorer people lived." (p. 181) While the author's description of this neighborhood (pp. 181 - 2) recalls to memory the people as well as the places Macon Dead II in Toni Morrison's *Song of Solomon* does not want to identify with, what seems to attract Dr Meadows's attention more than anything else is "a dark-skinned man with a cap yanked low over an unruly bush…" This man, whom Dr Meadows is quick to type "Welfare Man," is posited as a contrasting entity destined to point to the fact that Dr Meadows's blackness needs some extra rhetoric to make it fully valid and acceptable. The mode of representation used by the author is almost exclusively the description, from different angles, of the physical, and human environment that Dr Meadows is a part of in Claybourne. Little wonder that when eventually one conversation does take place, it carries a lot of weight. When Dr Meadows, under the spell of his "supermarket memories," tramples the dark-skinned man's feet, he (Meadows) is woken up to the realities of his racial status:

> "Watchit, honky!"
>
> Honky! You mutherfuckin dumb bastard, don't
> You know a Blood when you see one?"
>
> Get the fuck off my feet, whatever the fuck
> You are."
>
> Two more men were coming out of the doorway.
> Then a woman with half her hair pressed and the other half raw
> came onto the porch, children
> Swarming all around her hips.
>
> "You on the wrong side of town, buddy." (p. 185)

Dr Meadows is an invisible black man in a black neighbourhood. He is perceived by "his" people as the "other" that is to say, and intruder out to disturb the community's peace of mind. His blackness cannot be acknowledged until he demands it. And even when he does demand it, it is not granted automatically:

> They were studying him. By now, they'd know he was not a honky. He felt himself coming into focus for them, like the movie stars on the lids of Dixie Cups he'd licked long ago into being. Coming into view for them now, his red gold-hair of no less than five grades – curly in front, stringy in back, wavy around the ears, slick on top, and downright nappy at the center. The barbers always went at the nigger hair with clippers ablaze but couldn't bear to clip the curls or shorten the back no matter how he instructed. Haircuts were a freak show. He licked his lips and tried to be patient. Now the grain of his skin would be coming into view, like a 35 mm blowup. He was never more clear to himself than when Black people examined

him this way, suspicious. He felt his nostrils flatten. For all his mother's pinching, his nose splayed out into his cheekbones now as if for the first time, as though willed. (…) They were satisfied he was one of them, he sensed. Though he wasn't fool enough to think being a nigger saved him.

Dr Meadows' reception inside the black community does not, at first sight, agree with his proclaimed role as a consciousness-raiser, which is why he laments the fact that his people fail to heed a "teacher" and a "synthesizer" like him, "come to prepare you for the transformation, (…) to forge the new alliances, (…) to throw open the new footpaths…" (p. 126)

That Dr Meadows always ends up being accepted in the community just as Obie – despite the difficulties they all have relating to the group, bears witness to the power and the healing possibilities that Toni Cade Bambara locates in the political cohesion of the black community.

CONCLUSION

In this study my concern has been to shed light on some of the many ways the creative writers Toni Morrison, Alice Walker, and Toni Cade Bambara represent black men in a selection of their early works. In each of the three chapters I have tried, first of all, to establish that all three writers, on a very general plane, portray their "brothers" against the background of a somewhat similar ideological project – black feminism. I have not, however, suggested any personal definition of black feminism which is very close to Alice Walker's womanism. Instead, I have simply paid close attention, on the one hand, to some critical essays by the very authors discussed, and on the other hand, I have depended substantially on the writings of other (black) feminist theorists for my understanding of the individual works. Because of the social status of most black American women since slavery, and also in light of the irony behind Barbara Smith's concept of black women as "double nonentities,"[76] I regard them as a cultural minority of a dispossessed minority. As a cultural entity, they account for their life experiences through the medium of their own language.

Toni Morrison, Alice Walker, and Toni Cade Bambara as I have considered them, belong to a tradition of black female novelists. Politics, economics, race, and gender combine to define the framework within which black men are "constructed" by their novelist sisters. In all the novels and short stories that I have studied, successive images of black men are revealed to the reader through a series of double features, namely the men's objectives as defined by the authors on the one hand, and on the other hand the psychological as

---

76 Barbara Smith:"Toward a black feminist criticism", in Judith Newton and Deborah Rosenfelt, eds. *Feminist Criticism and Social Change*. New York: Methuen), 1985, p. 6.

well as intellectual energies the authors have these men mobilize in view of reaching the objectives thus defined.

Toni Morrison, more often than not, sees each of these objectives as the starting point of a freely chosen route that black men think will lead them to self-fulfillment. She repeatedly creates tension between the goal and the definer's self-evaluation. Cholly's marriage to Pauline, and their journey up north, Milkman's journey down south, Macon Dead II's commitment to the acquisition of material things, and Son's rejection of whatever Jadine stands for are just few examples of the moments when these tensions are given shape and expression. The women in their lives often deflect the course of these men's progress or keep quiet and, as a result of their silence, spur their men as the latter engage in courting confusion and chaos. Whenever men project their dreams into the future, they tend to ignore both the destructive and the constructive capabilities of black women's inner force.

Alice Walker tends exclusively to depict in her novels black men who achieve a sense of self-accomplishment only when they keep women "in their proper place." Her black men are petrified by the prospect of any relationship in which a (black) woman is to be perceived as an equal partner. The younger Grange Copeland, Brownfield Copeland, Truman Held, and Mr_ all experienced these feelings or were traumatized by similar ones. To avoid the trauma, most of the male characters in Alice Walker's fictional world eventually develop a coping system sustained by a central attitude that basically proclaims that the more a man wants to be, the farther down he must keep a woman. Alice Walker's fiction thrives on the recurring irony that, morally speaking, the men who push the female characters into the ditch end up hanging around the ditch because this is the only way the "pushers" can make sure that the "pushed" do not come out of the ditch or rise into a new threat. Even when Alice Walker tries hard to redeem a male character already compromised – as she does in the cases of the older Grange and the older Albert – most of the reader's original bitterness with the "villain" remains.

The power conflict which openly cripples blacks' married lives in novels such as Toni Morrison's *The Bluest Eye*, or Alice Walker's *The Third Life of Grange Copeland*, is handled in a more subtle way in the world of Toni Cade Bambara's stories. Bambara insists in her fiction that black men can play a very positive political role reconstructing the black community – only if they realize the determining importance of black women's contribution. She envisions a future where black male ego can keep on asserting itself without having, as a prerequisite, to shut down black women.

However, the truth of the matter remains that Morrison, Walker, and Bambara write primarily about black women. The black man, as he appears in these women's creative works is, therefore, just one of the various means used by these authors to drive home the urgency for the black woman to start reconstructing her shattered self. Unfortunately, the re-conquest – as well as the re-affirmation – by the black woman of her psychological integrity and her intellectual dignity happens almost exclusively during her encounter with the black man in the process of giving up his socio-historically defined old self for a new self-involved in a love-hate relationship with the American Dream. In the fiction of Toni Morrison, Alice Walker, and Toni Cade Bambara the black man engages in a "rite of passage" he may not complete until he fully acknowledges, and pays all due respect to, the thinking presence – in his life – of the black woman.

Selected bibliography

The corpus

Morrison, Toni. *The Bluest Eye*. New York: Washington Square Press, 1972, 1970.
-------- *Sula*. New York: New American Library, 1982, 1973.
-------- *Song of Solomon*. New York: New American Library, 1978, 1977.
-------- *Tar Baby*. New York: Alfred A. Knopf, 1981.
Walker, Alice. *The Third Life of Grange Copeland*. New York: Harcourt Brace Jovanovich, 1970.
-------- *Meridian*. New York: Washington Square Press, 1977, 1976.
-------- *The Color Purple*. Washington Square Press, 1983, 1982.
Bambara, Toni Cade. *Gorilla My Love*. New York: Random House, 1972.
-------- *The Sea Birds Are Still Alive*. New York: Vintage Books (Random House), 1982, 1977.
-------- *The Salt Eaters*. New York: Vintage Books (Random House), 1981, 1980.

Secondary Sources

Baker, Jr., Houston A. *The Journey Back*. Chicago: The University of Chicago Press, 1980, 1983.
-------- *Blues, Ideology, and Afro-American Literature*. Chicago: The University of Chicago Press, 1984.
Baldwin, James. *The Price of the Ticket*. New York: St. Martin's /Marek, 1985.
Bambara, Toni Cade. "What It Is I think I'm Doing Anyhow," in Janet Sternburg, ed. *The Writer on Her Work*. New York.: W. W. Norton and Company, 1980, pp. 153 - 168.
Baraka, Amiri. *Home*. New York: Morrow, 1966.
-------- "Afro-American Literature and Class Struggle," in Black American Literature Forum, Vol. 14, Number 1, Spring 1980, pp. 5 - 14.
Barton, Rebecca Chalmers. *Black Voices in American Fiction: 1900 - 1930*. Oakdale, New York: Dowling College Press, 1976.
Berghahn, Marion. *Images of Africa in Black American Literature*, Totowa, N. J., Rowman and Littlefied, 1977.
Bruck, Peter and Wolfang Karrer, eds. *The Afro-American Novel Since 1960*. Amsterdam: Gruner, 1982.
Byerman, Keith E. *Fingering the Jagged Grain: Tradition and Form in Recent Black Fiction*. Athens and London: The University of Georgia Press, 1985.
Cade, Toni, ed. *The Black Woman: An Anthology*. New York: New American Library, 1970.

Christian, Barbara. *Black Women Novelists*. Westport, Conn.: Greenwood Press, 1980.
--------, *Black Feminist Criticism*, New York: Pergamon, 1985.
Cooke, Michael G. *Afro-American Literature in the Twentieth Century*. New Haven: Yale University Press, 1984.
Cooley, John R. *Savages and Naturals*. London and Toronto: Associated University Press, 1982.
Cruse, Harold. *The Crisis of the Negro Intellectual*. New York: William Morrow and Company, 1967, 1970.
Davis, Charles T. *Black is the Color of the Cosmos*. New York: Garland Publishing, Inc., 1982.
Dubois, W. E. B. *The Souls of Black Folk*. Greenwich, Con,: Fawcett Publications, 1903, 1961.
Ellison, Ralph. *Shadow and Act*. New York: Random House, 1964.
-------- "Remembering Richard Wright," in Delta, Num. 18, April 1984, pp. 1 - 15.
Evans, Mari, ed. *Black Women Writers*. Garden City, N. Y.: Anchor Books, 1984.
Ford, Nick Aaron. *The Contemporary Negro Novel*. College Park, Md.: McGrath Publishing Company, 1968.
Gates, Jr., H. L., ed. *Black Literature and Literary Theory*. New York: Methuen, 1984.
Gayle, Jr., Addison. *Black Expression*. New York: Weybright and Talley, 1969.
--------, *The Way of the New World*. New York: Doubleday, 1975.
Genovese, E. D. *Roll, Jordan, Roll*. New York: Vintage Books, 1972, 1976.
Giddings, Paula. *When and Where I enter*. New York: W. Morrow, 1984.
Goldstein, R. L., ed. *Black Life and Culture in the United States*. New York: Thomas Y. Cromwell Company, 1971.
Grier, W. H. and Price Cobbs. *Black Rage*. New York: Bantam Books, 1968, 1969.
Gross, Seymour L. and J. E. Hardy, eds. *Images of the Negro in American Literature*. Chicago: The University of Chicago Press, 1966.
Halliday, M.A.K. *Language as Social Semiotic: The Social Interpretation of Language and Meaning*. Edward Arnold, Baltimore, Maryland, 1987
--------------------. *Cohesion in English*. Longman, London, 1976
Harris, Trudier. Exorcising Blackness. Bloomington: Indiana University Press, 1984.
--------------------. "On *The Color Purple*, Stereotypes, and Silence," in *Black American Literature Forum*, Vol. 18, Number 4, Winter 84, pp. 155-161.
Hemenway, Robert, ed. *The Black Novelist*. Columbus, Ohio: Charles E. Merrill Publishing Company, 1970.
Hughes, Carl Milton. *The Negro Novelist*. New York: The Citadel Press, 1953.
Gates, Jr., Henry Louis. *Figures in Black: Words, Signs, and the "Racial" Self*, Oxford University Press, 1987
Jones, LeRoi. *Blues People*. New York: W. Morrow and Company, 1963.
Karon, Bertram. *The Negro Personality*. New York: Springer Publishing Co. Inc., 1958.

Klotman, Paillis Rauch. *Another Man Gone*. Port Washington & London: Kennikat Press, 1963.
Ladner, Joyce A. *Tomorrow's Tomorrow*. New York: Anchor Books, 1971.
Levine, Lawrence, W. *Black Culture and Black Consciousness*. New York: Oxford University Press, 1977.
Locke, Alain, ed. *The New Negro*. New York: Antheneum, 1925, 1977.
Laorde, Audre. *Sister Outsider*. Trumansburg, N. Y.: The Crossing Press Feminist Series, 1984.
Miller, Jane. *Women Writing About Men*. New York: Pantheon Books, 1986.
Miller, R. Baxter, ed. *Black American Literature and Humanism*. Lexington, Ky.: The University Press of Kentucky, 1981.
Ogunyemi, Chikwenye Okonjo: "*Sula*: 'A Nigger Joke,'" in *Black American Literature Forum*, Vol. 14, Number 4, Winter 79.
Ostendorf, Berndt. *Black Literature in White America*. New Jersey: Barnes and Noble Books, 1982.
Page, Monte M., ed. *Personality: Current Theory and Research*. Lincoln, Nebraska: University of Nebraska Press, 1983.
Pryse, M. and Hortense J. Spillers, ed. *Conjuring*. Bloomington: Indian University, 1985.
Showalter, Elaine, ed. *The New Feminist Criticism*. New York: Pantheon, 1985.
Staples, Robert. *The Black Woman in America*. Chicago: Nelson Hall, Publishers, 1973.
Starke, Catherine Juanita. *Black Portraiture in American Fiction*. New York: Basic Books Inc., 1971.
Singh, Amritjit. *The Novels of the Harlem Renaissance*. University Park and London: The Pennsylvania State University Press, 1976.
Tate, Claudia, ed. *Black Women Writers at Work*. New York: Continuum, 1983.
Trischler, Nancy M. *Black Masks*. University Park and London: The Pennsylvania State University Press, 1969.
Turner, Darwin T. *In a Minor Chord*. Carbondale: Southern Illinois University Press, 1971.
Wade-Gayle, Gloria. *No Crystal Stair*. New York: The Pilgrim Press, 1984.
Walker, Alice. *In Search of Our Mother's Garden*. New York: Harcourt Brace Jovanovich, 1983.
Whittow, Roger. *The Darker Vision*. New York: Gordon Press, 1977.
Williams, Sherley Anne. *Give Birth to Brightness*. New York: The Dial Press, 1972.
Willis, Susan. "Eruptions of Funk: Historicizing Toni Morrison," in *Black American Literature Forum*, Vol. 16, Number 1, Spring 1982.

www.ingramcontent.com/pod-product-compliance
Lightning Source LLC
Chambersburg PA
CBHW070832300426
44111CB00014B/2529